PORTRAITS *of* Freedom

14 People

Who Came Out of

Homosexuality

Bob Davies
with Lela Gilbert

InterVarsity Press
Downers Grove, Illinois

The stories in this book are true. In some cases, however, minor details have been altered to protect the identity of family members, former spouses, and other persons in the stories.

InterVarsity Press
P.O. Box 1400, Downers Grove, IL 60515-1426
World Wide Web: www.ivpress.com
E-mail: mail@ivpress.com

InterVarsity Press® is the book-publishing division of InterVarsity Christian Fellowship/USA®, a student movement active on campus at hundreds of universities, colleges and schools of nursing in the United States of America, and a member movement of the International Fellowship of Evangelical Students. For information about local and regional activities, write Public Relations Dept., InterVarsity Christian Fellowship/USA, 6400 Schroeder Rd., P.O. Box 7895, Madison, WI 53707-7895.

Barbara Swallow's story is adapted from the book Free Indeed *by Barbara Swallow with Terry Murphy (Exodus Publishing, 2000). Used by permission.*

Cover photograph: © Kaz Chiba/Photonica

ISBN 0-8308-2331-X

Printed in the United States of America ∞

Library of Congress Cataloging-in-Publication Data

Davies, Bob, 1951-
  Portraits of freedom: fourteen people who came out of homosexuality/Bob Davies
  with Lela Gilbert.
    p. cm.
  ISBN 0-8308-2331-X
  1. Christian biography—United States. 2. Homosexuality—Religious
aspects—Christianity. I. Gilbert, Lela. II. Title.
BR1702 .D38 2001
261.8'35766'0922—dc21
  [B]   *2001024036*

| 20 | 19 | 18 | 17 | 16 | 15 | 14 | 13 | 12 | 11 | 10 | 9 | 8 | 7 | 6 | 5 | 4 | 3 |
| 17 | 16 | 15 | 14 | 13 | 12 | 11 | 10 | 09 | 08 | 07 | 06 | 05 | 04 | | | | |

To the thousands of ex-gay men and women worldwide,
whose lives are beautiful portraits of God's glory and power

Contents

Introduction

Can homosexuals change? Or is homosexuality inborn and, therefore, not subject to change?

Few subjects arouse such strong feelings in the church today as this one. In the past thirty years homosexuality has gone from a silent issue rarely mentioned to a central issue that is debated within many churches and denominations.

It seems as if everyone has an opinion. Some conservative churches wish the issue would disappear and still refuse to address it publicly. Other evangelical churches find a growing number of strugglers in their midst to whom they wish to offer a compassionate, biblical response. But they are not sure what to say or do. Other parishes, commonly called "liberal" or "moderate," offer an open door of welcome to practicing homosexuals and lesbians who wish to embrace both their Christian faith and their same-sex relationships.

All of these groups claim biblical support for their particular positions. Is it any wonder that opinions vary widely on this subject in today's churches?

The Ex-Gay Movement
In the past twenty-five years, as thousands of homosexuals and lesbians have "come out of the closet" to declare their homosexuality,

another group of people has also come into public view. They are *ex-gays*, a distinct and relatively unseen minority, a subgroup from within the gay community. These former homosexuals and lesbians have another viewpoint. They claim that they have left homosexuality for the sake of a higher calling, as an act of obedience to the Bible, which they believe declares that homosexual behavior is outside God's will. And many of them claim that they have changed in the deepest part of their beings, including their sexual feelings.

Who are these people? And what are they really like outside of the public spotlight? Stories of their testimonies of healing and deliverance from homosexuality circulate in magazines and on the Web, but many Christians have never met anyone who has actually left homosexuality behind. What is the real story here? Have these people really changed? Are they ex-gay, gay or straight? What are their relationships like with the opposite sex? Do they still experience same-sex attractions? If so, how do they reconcile that reality with their claim to have experienced some kind of change? Are they kidding themselves? Or have they experienced a valid transformation that bears a closer examination?

Furthermore, some of these men and women are now married with families. Are their marriages healthy? Do they have an active sex life within their marriages? Or do they live with an opposite-sex "roommate" with no romantic interaction for social approval or other motives?

There are many questions—and this book provides many answers. In the coming chapters we relate the stories of fourteen men and women. These testimonies offer a firsthand glimpse behind the scenes into the joys and ongoing struggles of their lives. You may be surprised by what you see and hear. In fact, before going further, here is an overview of what you will see firsthand in these stories.

"Healing" from Homosexuality

First, you will discover immediately that "healing" from homosexuality is not the simple, straightforward process that some people might believe. Real life is rarely as easy as theoretical answers. Coming out of homosexuality—especially when it has been a central pillar of someone's identity for many years—is usually a complex process that occurs over a number of years. In fact, most ex-gays bear witness to the fact that it is one of the most difficult challenges they have ever attempted in their Christian journey.

Why is this? Because homosexuality itself is complex. Debates still rage about the causes of this condition. In Christian circles the central question is often presented this way: Is homosexuality inborn or chosen?

Our response: Neither—at least, not in those simplistic terms.

Few homosexuals ever remember making a conscious choice to experience same-sex attractions. As you will read in these stories, it's common for homosexual feelings simply to be there as a person enters the teen years, especially for men. Some women become aware of lesbian feelings much later in life, even after entering into a heterosexual marriage. Many men and women who have experienced some same-sex attractions think that marriage will resolve them, but this is rarely true.

Other men and women wonder if they are simply going through a phase that they will outgrow. Don't most kids experiment sexually during childhood or in their early teens? Or, at least, don't most people have same-sex dreams or fleeting desires that ultimately mean nothing and are soon forgotten? Many ex-gays can tell stories of exploring their childhood or pubescent sexual feelings with another friend. Later the friend moves on to happy heterosexuality and marriage. The ex-gay is left with secret longings and desires, awakened by the experience, which continue to disturb and disrupt his or her life.

There is still ongoing research into the causes behind the homosexual condition. We won't provide an in-depth overview here. There are many other excellent books that explore this topic in detail (see our list of resources at <www.exodusnorthamerica.org>). However, we think that in reading the following stories you will recognize many life patterns, which will be instructive. In our experience of knowing hundreds of men and women who have left homosexuality, we have seen many common themes woven through their early-life experiences. At Exodus International we believe that homosexuality is a surface symptom of more deeply rooted spiritual and emotional issues that must be resolved in order to see real and lasting change. The root issues vary from individual to individual. But there are many common roots—and you will see them growing in the lives of the men and women profiled in this book. Here are a few of the most common that you'll see throughout the coming chapters:

Lack of same-sex intimacy. This is especially true for the male homosexual. Many boys who become gay in adulthood remember feeling different from other boys. They lacked strong same-sex friendships. They struggled with same-sex peer relationships. In many cases, fathers and father figures were physically absent or emotionally unavailable.

Lack of security in one's gender role. Numerous men and women recall feelings of doubt about being a *real* boy or a *real* girl. They may have engaged in activities commonly associated with the opposite sex, such as boys playing with dolls and girls being labeled "tomboys" for climbing trees and playing war games. Name-calling and labeling are common in childhood—and these people received more than their share of it.

Abuse by men. The overwhelming majority of ex-gay women report that they suffered abuse by men in their formative years. Usually this was sexual abuse, but emotional and verbal abuses are also extremely common. This abuse caused these women to reject men as potential emotional and romantic partners.

For ex-gay men, sexual abuse is also a relatively common background factor. Being abused by an older man caused these young boys to question their sexual identity, and sometimes these experiences awakened the same-sex urges that they later embraced in adulthood as a gay identity.

These types of childhood events may or may not have *caused* homosexuality. However, we believe that they provided the fertile ground where homosexual desires later took root.

The Change Process

Ultimately this question of where homosexuality arises is important because an analysis of the "problem" points to possible solutions. If homosexuality is truly genetic, then the question of change is difficult, if not impossible. However, the reality of change in the lives of many individuals points to a different understanding of this condition.

Most of these stories are from people who have been involved in Exodus-affiliated ministries. This is not to say that Exodus has the only successful ministry with ex-gays or that people don't leave homosexuality in other ways. However, these are the stories that *we* know and are, therefore, the stories that we can tell honestly and simply. You will also see again and again that the change process was usually motivated by a spiritual conviction that homosexuality was wrong and against the will of a sovereign God. Often God intervened in subtle or dramatic ways in people's lives to motivate them to undertake this change. All of the stories in this book involve believers who sought God's help in leaving homosexuality behind.

We should also take a moment to explain that we are not discussing a change in behavior as the answer to overcoming homosexuality. Simply stopping a certain behavior resolves little. It can be an important first step in the change process, but it is not the whole process itself. And, as you will read in the pages that follow, even achieving this first step can be a huge challenge for men and women who have become addicted to certain sexual behaviors. Nevertheless, comparatively speaking, this action of changing one's sexual behavior is one of the easiest steps to attain—and something being lived out daily in the lives of thousands of former homosexuals and lesbians.

Yes, stopping homosexual acting out is an important first step. But what then? Even more difficult issues are next: experiencing change in thoughts and sense of self. These are the deepest root issues that must change in order for a person to experience the deepest possible sense of freedom from his or her homosexual background. And these areas are the most stubborn and difficult to change.

Changing thoughts and sexual attractions goes deeper than behavior and takes longer to become a reality. In fact, the area of thoughts, attractions and temptations is probably the area of greatest challenge—and the widest variety of experience—among former gays and lesbians. Some people, even after years of spiritual effort, have experienced relatively little change in their sexual attractions. Others have experienced a great deal of change, which has opened the door to pursuing heterosexual marriage and parenthood. A growing number of ex-gays are now happily raising a generation of children whose very existence counters the idea that gays cannot change, at least in behavior.

We do not believe, by the way, that marriage and family should be the ultimate goal of ex-gay counseling. There are no guarantees where one will eventually find himself or herself after entering this process. Many ex-gays are single—and much more satisfied and peaceful than when they were involved in a gay partnership. Marriage is not the proof of healing; all ex-gay ministries can tell you that they receive frequent pleas for help from married men and women who are thoroughly entrenched in homosexuality. In short, a marriage license guarantees nothing in terms of freedom from same-sex attractions.

But, even though it is difficult, many ex-gays know that it is not impossible to experience a radical shift in one's sexual attractions. The change may not be swift or complete, but it is still real. Many former homosexuals admit to ongoing temptation of one sort or another, but they bear witness to the fact that the power and frequency of the same-sex attractions have diminished significantly.

And they expect that, as they continue in their healing process, further and even deeper changes will occur in their thought life.

Ultimately the deepest change occurs in a person's core identity. Particularly in light of the modern gay-rights movement, being gay or lesbian has become the center of many people's identities. This is their defining hallmark. Their sexuality is the lens through which all experiences are filtered. They may even live in a gay subculture, where all their friends are gay. Their local shops are gay-owned. Their church is gay-affirmative. Their coworkers are gay. Their magazines and books are gay. Their entire worldview is gay.

Identity—the core sense of who I am—is the deepest and most difficult area to experience change. It is especially confusing if a person continues to experience gay feelings.

This is where the reality of the Scriptures can have its most powerful effect. Am I defined by my feelings or by who God says that I am? For all Christians, there is an ongoing struggle between flesh and spirit that is a daily reality. Which of these two natures is the real me? More to the point, what does this inner conflict signify for the person leaving homosexuality?

For the Christian, overcoming his or her past—whether homosexuality or some other life-dominating struggle—is an ongoing process of spiritual growth. In one sense, it never ends. It's a lifelong endeavor that continues until we see Christ face to face. And the transformation that the former homosexual is undergoing is essentially a maturing experience similar to that of any believer. The journey out of homosexuality is not unique—it just has different views along the way from that of the average heterosexual seeking healing from his or her past.

Think of overcoming homosexuality as a long hike. After one hour you may be deep in the forest or surrounded by other obstacles that prevent you from seeing too far ahead on the trail. Have you arrived? Not yet. But have you made progress? Definitely! This is a similar place to where many ex-gays find themselves after a significant period of counseling and spiritual support in leaving homosexuality.

This idea of a *long process* causes some problems. For one thing, it can be discouraging to those contemplating the journey. Have you ever gone on a hike and felt totally winded after about fifteen minutes? Perhaps the first part of the trail is a steep upgrade. You feel tired after walking only ten minutes. But as you persist, you can experience the common phenomenon of a second wind, and your energy is renewed and replenished as you keep walking.

Similarly, some former homosexuals become deeply discouraged after only a few months of counseling. Perhaps they came into the process with wrong expectations. They expected to be much further along by this time. Where is God? And why isn't this becoming any easier?

The Issue of Expectations

The whole issue of expectations is an important one. If you begin a hike that is marked easy in the guidebook and find that you are exhausted after several miles, you will probably become discouraged or even angry. Your initial expectations have proven to be false. Now what? You can either keep walking or turn back.

Like any recovery type of ministry, a significant number of men and women turn back in discouragement after walking along the ex-gay pathway for a season. Some of them have been out of homosexual behavior for years. Their decision to return to the old and familiar ways can cause discouragement among others who have looked to them for inspiration and leadership. Why do people turn back?

In some cases, these people's expectations are false or unrealistic. Often the journey out of homosexuality is harder and longer than they had ever imagined. After a certain time period—say six months or a year—they are discouraged to see how little progress has apparently been made. *At this rate,* they wonder, *how long will it take before I experience any degree of significant change in this area of my life?*

Others have unconsciously chosen a trial period during which they will attempt change. When certain things don't happen within that period, they give up. Maybe they had secretly entered a counseling situation with high hopes of being married. After two years marriage appears as far in the future as ever. So they give up. "This didn't work for me," they sigh, returning to same-sex romance to satisfy their needs for companionship.

Others enter counseling with the goal and expectation that *all* homosexual feelings will cease after a certain time period. When this is not attained after several years of effort, they grow discontent and eventually give up.

So a person's motives for even getting involved in ex-gay ministry need to be examined. What is the goal? What are the real reasons for entering counseling? Many former homosexuals tell us that there is only one genuine reason that they have been successful: they have abandoned homosexuality in obedience to God's Word. They see changing their homosexuality as a side effect of an even bigger goal: being conformed to the image of Jesus Christ.

One former homosexual said, "My prayer since the day I entered ex-gay ministry has been the same: 'Lord, make me into the man of God that you created me to be.'" This man, now married for fifteen years, did not come into counseling with the primary goal of becoming straight. He wanted to experience more of God's fullness in his life. He wanted to grow emotionally, spiritually and in every other way. He wanted to experience life in all its richness, as Jesus promised in the Scriptures: "I have come that you might have life, and have it to the full" (John 10:10).

An Unsatisfying Way of Life

Thousands of men and women come to Exodus ministries seeking help in leaving homosexuality because they have found same-sex relationships to be ultimately disappointing and less than totally fulfilling. They sense there is something more that is available, and they want it.

Most also come from a prior conviction that the Bible condemns homosexual acts, so they have decided to submit their lives to that edict, even if they don't fully understand the whole *why* of God's declaration that gay sex is sinful.

The problem some of these men and women experience is that, partway through the healing journey, they begin to forget the painful side of their past homosexual involvement and focus only on the pleasurable times. They begin to experience a longing for the "good old days." They remember the camaraderie, the deep sense of family and fellowship that they experienced with other members of the gay community.

Perhaps some of them are experiencing disappointments in straight society. Particularly painful are some church-related experiences. All too often Christian men and women who should be giving support and expressing love withdraw in condemnation and fear when someone's ex-gay past becomes known in the church. Sadly, there are still far too few safe churches where former homosexuals and lesbians can be open about their past sins and find support for their current struggles.

The fact is, simply seeking a straight lifestyle is a flawed motive for abandoning homosexuality in the first place. The ultimate goal should be reaching spiritual maturity, not experiencing a certain sexual orientation. Then, if same-sex desires do not change as quickly as one had hoped, or if opposite-sex feelings do not arise as powerfully as one had imagined, there will still be a deeper motivation for staying on the pathway toward wholeness.

The Call of the Cross

No matter what our particular struggles may be, the direction for all of us as Christian disciples is the same. Jesus challenges us to "take up [our] cross" and follow him (Matthew 16:24). Whether our cross is same-sex attractions or some other unbiblical pull of the flesh, we are called to crucify those desires and turn willingly toward Christ.

Remarkably, there is evidence for change from homosexuality right in the New Testament church. In speaking to the Corinthian believers, the apostle Paul said that some of them had been involved in various sinful lifestyles, including homosexuality. But then he declared, "And that is what some of you were. But you were washed, you were sanctified, you were justified in the name of the Lord Jesus Christ and by the spirit of our God" (1 Corinthians 6:11).

Coming out of homosexuality is not a new phenomenon. It has been occurring in the church since the days of the first-century church—if not before. The message of hope for overcoming homosexuality has been declared for many centuries. And with the rise of the modern gay-rights movement, it is being demonstrated ever more frequently through the lives of thousands of ex-gay men and women around the world.

Political Implications

Finally, the testimonies in the following chapters are not given here primarily to win any political or public policy debates. For one thing, the black-and-white mentality of many political skirmishes has sometimes obscured the complexity of the real issues.

"These men and women have changed. So you can too!" Christians shout to the gay community.

"But they are still tempted. So they haven't changed at all!" retort the gay activists.

Neither position truly represents the complex reality of what ex-gay men and women generally experience in their daily lives.

The political implications of the whole subject have contributed to the heat surrounding this issue. The modern gay-rights movement is firmly built upon several key ideas, including the one that homosexuality is genetic and therefore cannot be changed. Some gay activists attempt to discredit ex-gay testimonies at any opportunity. They protest when any financial contributions are given to ex-gay causes. And they engage in expensive counter-public relations campaigns when ex-gay activities or claims are advertised nationally.

The statement "I'm ex-gay" has political implications. We understand that—yet that reality alone is not sufficient reason for us to keep our stories hidden. We must share the truth about homosexuality, wherever that truth leads us. Although many ex-gays are not particularly interested in political debates surrounding the issue of homosexuality, the fact that their stories exist generates considerable debate among political activists.

Purposes of This Book

With that in mind we hope this book will serve several purposes. First, if you are interested in exploring the possibility of leaving homosexuality, these stories will encourage you that change is possible—as well as challenging. Deeply ingrained habits change slowly and with great difficulty.

Second, if you have a loved one involved in homosexuality or who has expressed an interest in the possibility of change, this book gives you insights into some of the key issues that must be faced in finding real and lasting change.

Third, this book gives you real-life illustrations of how you can help someone involved in the change process. Few ex-gay men and women have experienced change in this area of their lives as "lone ranger" Christians. In almost every case, change has involved the friendship and prayers of other believers who came alongside to offer emotional and spiritual support.

Fourth, we believe that this book can also have important implications for parents of young children. As you read about the individuals who have agreed to share their stories, you will see many common childhood struggles that were early signposts of later difficulties with same-sex attractions. We believe that when these symptoms of gender confusion exist in children, if appropriate intervention is taken, the chances of the child's growing up to experience homosexuality can be greatly reduced.

With this in mind we introduce to you fourteen individuals whose *Portraits of Freedom* we hope you will find illuminating, spiritually encouraging and thought provoking. These people are not perfect, and we have tried to honestly present their stories, warts and all. As you read, note that not all their choices were wise ones, even after they made the decision to follow Christ and leave homosexuality. All of our lives are a mixture of the exemplary and the foolish. So everything these people did or said should not necessarily be taken as a model for others. Rather, these stories offer an imperfect witness of God's power to change sinners into struggling saints in order to reflect his glory.

We hope and pray that they offer you a unique perspective, an inside look into one of the most important and controversial moral issues in our society.

1

Letting Go of Loneliness

Ann Phillips

*I*t was a beautiful late-spring Sunday. The windows in the house were open and a pleasant breeze off the Chesapeake Bay gently rustled the curtains. Yet that morning Ann Phillips could hardly breathe. The tremendous weight pressing against her chest seemed to be squeezing the life out of her.

What had she done? How could she have done such a thing? Now she would always be lonely. Ann had ended a lesbian partnership of nearly twenty years, and she was lying across her bed weeping, overwhelmed with pain and uncertainty.

Almost a year earlier Ann had received Jesus Christ into her heart. Since her conversion she had tried desperately to maintain her gay identity while pursuing a closer relationship with God. She had become actively involved in her religious denomination's pro-gay group. However, instead of receiving peace and a greater capacity to enjoy life, Ann felt as if she had placed herself in an enormous vice that was slowly being turned tighter and tighter.

Over several months she had found a multitude of books, organizations and even pastors who told her that homosexuality was acceptable for a Christian.

"It simply isn't sin," they told her. "God made you gay, and he doesn't make mistakes." Ann recalls her reaction:

Try as I might, I was never satisfied with their answers. The attitudes, activities and rhetoric of the pro-gay theology movement never seemed to line up with what I was reading in Scripture and hearing in my heart. So many of their positions seemed to be motivated by self-interest and anger. No one appeared to be particularly concerned that they or anyone else move closer to Christ. The focus was all about our getting acceptance and affirmation of our homosexuality from the church, regardless of the cost.

In time I didn't feel like I belonged within the gay subculture—Christian or otherwise—anymore, and yet I wasn't sure I fit in with conservative evangelicals either. Of course, I also read books and listened to pastors on the other side who said the life I had lived for almost twenty-three years was sinful and had to stop. Their words terrified me.

Inside I was screaming, "But I am gay and I am Christian—what would you have me to do?"

In response, it seemed as though God had hunted me down, and I was backed into a corner. Every fiber of my being had cried out to know the truth, but who could I believe when even the church seemed to disagree? The pressure I felt within me was incredible and unbearable. □

"But I *Am* Gay"

Approximately two weeks before that painful Sunday when she ended her lesbian relationship, Pastor Rod White had baptized Ann in the Gulf of Mexico. Before the baptism, while sitting in his office, the two of them had discussed homosexuality and Christianity. He said, "I hear you still call yourself gay."

Ann was seated across from him wearing a man's haircut and men's clothes. *What an odd statement,* she thought to herself. Aloud she simply replied, "But I *am* gay."

Quoting 2 Corinthians 5:17 Pastor Rod explained that when Ann became a Christian, she had also become a new person. "What you're telling me, Ann, is that you *feel* gay," he said.

Wow, these are some pretty powerful feelings then, she thought.

Pastor Rod picked up his Bible and started reading to her from Romans 6. He encouraged Ann to apply the entire sixth chapter of Romans to her own circumstances. Then he gave her what was soon to become the best advice she had ever received: "Quit reading all the books and read God's Word. Quit listening to all the preachers, including me, and listen for God's voice. Ann, I really do believe that you want to know the truth. And I know that God will honor that."

Pastor Rod knew that God had placed within Ann the desire to know the truth. But at that moment her emotions were kicking and screaming, begging her to remain in denial.

Nonetheless, for the next two weeks Ann read Romans 6 aloud every night. The words seemed to burn their way into her soul. Many nights she felt like throwing her Bible across the room, but she didn't. Instead she kept reading. For days Ann thought Paul's epistle to the Romans contained the cruelest words she had ever read.

I despised Pastor Rod for "making me" read them night after night. But since he was five hundred miles away, it was really the Holy Spirit who would not release me from those twenty-three verses. One night as I personalized the first and second verses, my heart finally heard the words I was speaking: "What shall I say then? Am I to continue in sin that grace might increase? God forbid! How shall I who died to sin still live in it?"

There it was—God's truth. For a solid year I had tried to rationalize, bargain, intellectualize and deny it away, but then I knew homosexuality was clearly a sin and no longer an option for me. Yet I was still at loose ends. I felt my homosexuality had me walled in on all sides with no escape. □

A few days later Ann ended up at a progay book study of a book called *Is the Homosexual My Neighbor?* The group was a mix of gay men, lesbians and pro-gay clergy.

People all around me were saying things like, "I didn't ask to be gay" and "I was born this way." These were statements I had made all my adult life. Then a woman seated right next to me made another comment I'd said many times: "And no one can change me."

Within my mind I heard these words crystal clear: But God can do anything. *There it was again—God's truth. He had a way out for me even if I couldn't imagine how this was possible. As much as I couldn't face leaving my partner and my gay identity, there was no alternative as far as I could see.* □

Ann's obedient reading of God's Word moved her closer to that day in June when she finally found the strength to break up with her partner. She had not planned to do so when she got out of bed that morning, but she could no longer tolerate living a lie now that she knew the truth. God was calling Ann to take a step of obedience, no matter how giant the step was.

In fact, in Ann's mind it was a step across a darkened Grand Canyon, but, somehow, for that one moment in time God gave her the strength she needed. She was well aware that once the choice was made, there would be no turning back. Outwardly she looked no different—her style was still decidedly masculine—and inwardly she felt like a wet dishcloth. But Ann was indeed changing. And now, like new wine, her reborn life could no longer stay in the old wineskin of the gay identity.

Not surprisingly Ann ran into a challenge almost immediately. Her first counselor following the breakup was a pastor who turned out to be progay. At first Ann did not know that he had a secret agenda to reunite her with her partner. He actually set Ann up in one session by having her former lover present. "The purpose," he explained, "is to help her grieve the breakup."

It soon became clear that was not his intention at all. Instead this pastor was trying to reconcile the two women, using his position, Ann's personal struggles and even Scripture as weapons against

Ann. Fortunately she found the strength to reject his efforts.

Facing the Specter of Loneliness

For some time after the breakup Ann was in a state of shock. It seemed that her actions had brought about her worst nightmare. She felt orphaned. As the only child of older parents she had always feared being alone. In those first moments and on into the coming months, her old nemesis loneliness shadowed her every move. Without warning, a heavy weight of alienation dropped over her like a thick winter blanket.

Since childhood Ann had anesthetized the pain of her isolation by spending hours upon hours in a fantasy world of her own design, populated by people of her own choosing. This behavior was seen as a praiseworthy ability to entertain herself for extended periods of time. While she was preoccupied with keeping herself busy, Ann set aside any need to connect with others. Despite her parents' overbearing need for her, she remained inordinately isolated. She describes her family environment:

I was an only child, and my parents much preferred me to each other. My father was a "dry drunk." He was very passive and childlike. I enjoyed his humor, playfulness and indulgence of me, but I felt insecure and unprotected by him emotionally, financially and sexually. While I have no recollection of my father sexually abusing me, I did sleep with him for some time until I complained to my mother. I knew my other friends' fathers did not sleep with them, and I felt ashamed and uncomfortable. I later learned this is a form of emotional-sexual abuse.

My father and mother were both emotionally incestuous with me. My mother had extreme, undiagnosed emotional issues. She was a "rage-aholic," extremely fearful and plagued with obsessive-compulsive behaviors. Both my father and I walked on eggshells around her. He never protected me from her nor did he ever stand up to her. She was emotionally and verbally abusive as well as very controlling. I was always afraid of her but saw her as more dependable than my father in the practical matters of my care.

I was very enmeshed with my mother from childhood into adulthood, not really knowing where she ended and I began. I always felt lonely, fearful and isolated as a child. Outwardly we seemed the happy little family. My parents idolized me and often told me they lived for me, but all that felt like a heavy burden.

We went to church simply because it was the right thing to do. If you'd asked my parents, they would probably have said that we were Christians, but we were not. In those days I saw no value in the church and no difference between so-called Christians and anyone else. □

All her life Ann had heard that her parents lived just for her. She was often reminded that because of her birth her father had given up years of drinking. In her mind Ann translated this message into a lifelong mandate: *It's your job to keep us alive and sober.*

Ann tried to become her mother's "perfect child," but in truth, she never quite measured up to the older woman's expectations. Her mother saw Ann as a mirror image of herself, while Ann longed to be known as herself, not a projection of someone else.

The mother isolated her daughter from what she perceived to be the negative influences of relatives. Ann was told that her extended family couldn't and shouldn't be trusted. In fact, her mother said that Ann couldn't trust anyone but her. Any relationship that took time or attention from Ann's mother was suspect and therefore discouraged.

Oddly enough, however, when Ann tried to move too close, in search of greater intimacy, her mother would pull away both physically and emotionally. Trying to explain this, she once told Ann, "You suffocate me." Early in her life Ann learned to hate her mother, vowing at a very young age never to be like her. In Ann's view all women were unpredictable, hypercritical and distant. And as for physical appearance, Ann's mother was a beautiful woman and very feminine. Ann consciously rejected anything that resembled that image.

Meanwhile, to her father Ann was a playmate in the fun times, an ally against her mother in difficult times and a surrogate spouse in lonely times. At some level Ann sensed that much of the affection and attention she received from both parents was more about them than about her. Her every material desire was met. She was never required to lift a finger. She apparently lived with two people whose lives revolved around her. Yet the constant specter of loneliness haunted her.

Ann continually retreated into never-ending daydreams. As an adult she continued to fantasize anytime her loneliness became too great. In her adult fantasies every woman desired her, and every man admired her because she was always brilliant, beautiful and brave.

Adding to her fantasy was Ann's discovery of pornography.

I was exposed to pornography at my aunt's house. Her sons kept it in the bathroom, and once I discovered it, every time I visited her house, I found a way to look at the magazines. I had an interest from that time forward. I really began to use it as a medication around 1982 or 1983. From that time on I used it constantly. It was very ritualistic for me, and, at the time, it dovetailed into my obsessive-compulsive disorder. It was also associated with compulsive masturbation. For me, pornography was really about isolation and loneliness. It was just another outgrowth from my childhood fantasy world. □

In the weeks following her turn from homosexuality, Ann's family and friends gradually heard the news about her decision. Her loneliness increased as angry letters and judgmental words attacked her motivations and even questioned her sanity. Her father had passed away years before, and her mother, who was nearing the end of her life, doubted Ann's ability to survive in the world without either her or Ann's ex-partner. The rest of the family was unable to help because years of disconnection had reduced them to virtual strangers. And finally, gay friends, who could not accept the direction her life had taken, rejected Ann. In Ann's mind she was utterly alone. She had no one.

Thankfully, God did not allow Ann's tears to blind her to his truth.

Friends to the Friendless

During this time a codependency support group at London Bridge Baptist Church rallied around her. Even before, while she was still involved in lesbianism, these "nice church ladies" had welcomed her into their fellowship. She had been warmly received as just another of the hungering and hurting. Since no one was an expert on homosexuality, they did all they knew to do—they loved her, encouraged her, prayed for her and trusted the Holy Spirit to change her.

But perhaps the greatest relief from isolation and a sense of abandonment came from a couple who worked in Ann's office. At first they and Ann seemed unlikely candidates to become friends. John and Pat Kulp represented everything Ann hated. They were conservative. They were Republicans. They were born-again Christians. They were prolife.

But Pat and Ann started to get to know each other during an aerobics class. Later Ann became Pat's manager at work. After three years Pat led Ann to Christ. From then on both Pat and John continued to disciple Ann, and when she left her partner and her homosexual behavior behind, she lived with them while she went through recovery.

Prior to my ending my lesbian relationship John and Pat Kulp and their family had prayed for me and witnessed to me for almost three years. After my conversion and decision to move away from homosexuality, they committed themselves to enter my battle for recovery. With patience, faithfulness, humor and compassion they never wavered from God's vision for me. In their eyes, I saw only a reflection of the woman God had ordained me to be before the beginning of time. While in therapy and a recovery program, I struggled through the swamp of emotional dependency, gender dis-identification, depression, pornography addiction and revelations of sexual-emotional abuse. These folks never retreated but slugged through it with me. □

After her graduation from the recovery program Ann lived with the Kulps for about eighteen months as they continued to instruct

her in life skills and the spiritual disciplines. Living in the safe environment of their home, she had both protection and accountability.
Stumbling blocks like cable access were removed, which made Ann
feel protected from the temptation of pornography. Areas like
appropriate female attire and manner obviously required accountability, but she also needed accountability in more subtle issues
such as time management.

*Pat and John have always believed in me. I truly think every person needs
someone in her life to believe in her—especially when there's not much to
believe in. They have been that for me as my spiritual parents and now my
friends. We are very close, and I thank God every day for them in my life.* □

Changes—Inside and Outside

Despite the Kulps' generosity of spirit, conflict was unavoidable.
Ann was both frightened and frustrated about her future. She had
tried to communicate with John and Pat but was unable to express
her pent-up emotions. Instead, one night she flew into a rage. She
found herself screaming in Pat's face—something she had never
done before. Part of her wanted to stop once she started, but
another part flew out of control. Her fear and frustration swelled to
bursting with every angry word.

After Ann's outburst Pat returned to the kitchen, and Ann continued vacuuming. Ann felt panicked, slamming the Hoover into
the walls and furniture. *I have really done it this time!* she thought. *I'm
going to find my bags in the front yard.* Ann felt an urge to run before
she was rejected.

Instead, moments later, Pat came into the room smiling. "We
need to talk," she told Ann.

Ann was shocked and confused by Pat's warm expression. As the
two women talked, Pat graciously acknowledged Ann's feelings.
She encouraged Ann, affirming that she saw within her the courage
and faith to walk through that difficult time. Amidst showers of
tears Ann apologized for her disrespectful behavior.

Later on Pat confided that as Ann had lashed out at her, God had showed Pat the image of a little child throwing a tantrum because she knew no other way to express her overwhelming emotions. "When I came back into the room," Pat explained, "I was determined to hear that child's feelings, but I was also going to speak truth into the grown woman standing before me."

Daily life in an interactive household forced Ann to deal with emotional issues such as fear, distrust, jealousy, dishonesty and self-ishness. And through John and Pat's godly responses, Ann's defects were firmly but respectfully confronted.

While she overcame her weaknesses, Ann also learned to refocus on the exercising of her strengths. Many times positive aspects of her character were recognized by the Kulps—traits that Ann could not yet see. Ann couldn't help but notice that the Kulps were excited by the work God was doing in her life. They cheered her on whether Ann was sprinting or crawling along in her spiritual journey.

One very special day Pat and her mother, Jackie, took me shopping. Because we would be looking for women's clothes and makeup, I was ready to have a miserable, humiliating time. At this point, everything feminine was still foreign to me. Just being in the ladies' department made me uncomfortable.

Instead of allowing me to feel humiliated, my friends tenderly coached me in styles and colors. As we laughed and talked together, I felt accepted as a woman. It was the first time I could ever remember not feeling somehow different and deficient. They rejoiced with me the following day when I ventured to church in my new outfit, makeup and earrings. With my "spiritual family," no victory was too small to celebrate, no wound too horrible to touch. □

God has since reconciled Ann to her family. Before her mother's death Ann asked forgiveness for the pain and shame her sin had caused. Ann thanked her mother for specific sacrifices her parents had made on their daughter's behalf. Since their passing, the Lord frequently reminds Ann of good memories and blessings that came to her through them. She recognizes that things like her passion for the arts, her devotion to learning and her love of nature are part of their legacy to Ann. "The same God who died on the cross for me," Ann reflects, "gave me the parents and the childhood I had for his own good purposes. And I am thankful."

For Ann, forgiveness has been a critical element for healing. It has come in stages for her. First has come an awareness of the offense. Then she has allowed herself to feel the offense's depth and intensity. Finally, she has chosen to release the person who committed the offense. "For me," Ann says, "there was no option. I had to forgive not just to thrive but to survive. Sometimes I think we forgive too quickly before allowing ourselves to grieve the offense. So for me it's been more of a process like removing layers of a callus to allow the new, raw skin underneath to heal."

When it came to forgiving her mother, Ann asked God to reveal to her who her mother really was in his eyes. How did God see her when she was at her worst—hurling insults, accusations, curses, guilt and manipulations Ann's way? He was faithful and gave to Ann the picture she needed. She saw a frightened, wounded child who felt powerless to defend herself against a very scary world. The Lord clearly had great compassion for her. And for the first time Ann felt a real love for her mother. She chose to be with her as she died, and their final moments together were sweet. This was so, even though the older woman really had not changed.

Soon more changes were in store for Ann, as God led her into leadership of the women's residential program at Love In Action, an Exodus ministry in Memphis.

After some five years of pouring the power of Jesus Christ into my life, the Kulps offered another compelling act of love by exhorting me to step back into the world on my own. Through the years of life-giving experience they shared with me, my belief in the residential recovery concept for homosexual strugglers took root. As I prayed for God's will and sought some way of giving back to others, I was drawn to the parallels between the Love In Action program and my own informal live-in experience.

Today I am single by circumstance. God gave me the desire sometime back to be married and have children. I am thankful for that, but I am also seeking to be willing to give that desire back to him should he require it. Right now I am the program director for women's ministry at Love In Action.

Over the years I have learned that the struggle homosexuals face is not really about leaving homosexuality or no longer feeling homosexual desires. It is about becoming more like Christ. We have to come to him with open hands even as it relates to our struggle. It's up to him whether he takes the feelings away or not. His grace is sufficient.

With him, I find loneliness can hold me captive less and less. The "Father to the fatherless" comforts me, delights in me. I've often considered people in homosexuality like relational and spiritual orphans. Throughout the years I have tried to note references to the orphaned in Scripture. God has made it clear to me that through him "the fatherless find compassion" (Hosea 14:3). In my life God has built a bridge, filling the chasm sin left and connecting me with him and his people. Our heavenly Father really does place the lonely in families, does set prisoners free, and does give them joy (Psalm 68:5-6). □

2

A Father Who Wants Me

Jim Shores

Jim Shores still vividly remembers the beginning of his journey into pain—which ultimately led him into homosexuality:

One Saturday, when I was eleven, my dad asked me if I'd like to go for a walk with him. I was thrilled because Dad never spent much time with me. I felt so proud as we walked down the street. This was my father, and I was his son. Then came the words I will never forget: "Jim, your mother and I have been having some problems . . ."

In a flash I realized where the conversation was headed. His request to spend time alone with me—for the first time in months—only served as a preamble to his leaving our lives for good.

I was furious. I was devastated. I cussed a blue streak at him before running away. How could my father leave me? Why didn't he spend any time with me? What was wrong with me? □

After that explosive conversation with his father, life—as young Jim knew it—would never again be the same. His father left home and moved in five houses down the street with Jim's mother's best friend. Jim started hating his dad and secretly realized that he had never really known his father in a deep way. Meanwhile, the family had shrunk from a very male club of five guys and a mom to one mom and an angry boy who had just entered puberty and junior high. Jim's oldest brothers were in college by then, and the third brother had gone to live with their dad. In Jim's words, "Life stunk."

Good News, Bad News

In the years before the divorce the Shores family had attended the First Methodist Church every Sunday and had shared a nice lunch at the country club afterwards. But the church attendance was perfunctory. No one in the family had a particularly deep faith during Jim's early years. His father was interested in various theories of evolution and, as it turned out later, was a practical atheist. Jim's mother had grown up as a believing Christian but had lost her zeal as an adult. Jim's childhood Sunday school classes taught him very little about sin and salvation. "Instead," Jim explains, "we learned about ecology, did crafts and learned that we should be nice to each other because God is love. That's about as deep as it got."

After the parents' separation, however, there was a huge spiritual change in the family. Jim and his mother became born-again Christians. In separate events within a year's time so did the other three brothers. The only remaining unbeliever was Jim's father, who was by then energetically embracing the maxim of the seventies: "If it feels good, do it."

Seeking to grow as Christians, Jim and his mother started going to a nondenominational Bible church. Jim began learning a lot about Scripture and found himself wondering why no one at First Methodist had ever explored the Bible. Later he understood. "The Bible demands change. You either have to ignore it or let it change you," he explains. "And most of those country clubbers were quite happy with the status quo." But Jim wasn't satisfied.

I needed help. And in God's Word I found assurances, promises, guidance and words to stand on. My relationship with God became one of son and father because there was no man standing in between him and me.

Even so, I desperately desired that there would be a man there for me, a father, someone under whose covering I could shelter, someone to interpret the world for me, explain to me the life changes I was going through in gentle, nurturing tones. I began to fantasize about who that man would be, if not my father.

At about this time I discovered my brothers' pornography—and not just a little but the mother lode. Down in the basement of our home was enough porn to cause a serious bump in the road for your average, garden-variety eleven year old. But I was by no means garden variety. I was desperately hungry for guidance. I felt alone, adrift, without a compass.

I had the Bible, but suddenly the Bible had a competitor. Once I discovered that pornography, a spirit of seduction crept into my life that would wreak havoc for years to come. A split developed between my world of faith and God, and my world of pornography, fantasy and masturbation. The magazines in the basement continued to provide solace. By age fourteen I was living a double life; part of me was devoted to God my Father, and the other part was equally devoted to pornographic images of men who were father, brother, friend and lover. □

Jim's father's absence wounded him deeply. And in this too he was divided. He both longed for his dad and hated him for leaving. In junior high, social rejection compounded Jim's woes. He was six foot four inches tall, rail thin, marred by acne and ill-fitting glasses, and terrified of sports. Because of his height Jim was easy prey for peers who were searching for someone to belittle. For a time, humiliation became Jim Shore's constant companion.

Stayin' Alive
But it wasn't long before Jim found a form of social salvation. The

latest dance rage was disco, and Jim discovered that he could dance—*really* dance—without inhibition, without fear. As he puts it, "I discovered I could be cute, I could be sexy, and, lo and behold, I babed out. You know what babing out is, don't you? That's when, in one summer during junior high or high school, you go from being the soul of dorkdom to a budding youth, full of promise—and attractive to girls."

A teen disco opened up next door to the high school. Without fail Jim was there every Friday and Saturday night. To his amazement girls were asking him to dance—popular girls. Jim was excited, thrilled and motivated. But something unexpected was happening to his relationships with girls. Again and again he was becoming their best friend.

How did that happen? Wasn't I supposed to date them? But no, I became their pal. What could it have been? My cologne? My hair? The fact that I was lusting over their boyfriends? Maybe it was the latter. Oh, I dated. But it always happened out of duty because it was the thing to do. I didn't know what to do with girls. I could talk to them intimately as friends. I could kiss and make out, and did so, and enjoyed it. But I always felt like an impostor.

Fact was, I had no idea how to simply, naturally combine my desire for intimacy with the world of women. Instead my desire for intimacy was targeted dead-on at the world of men. The male world was the one I felt I didn't belong to: a world of sports minus the fear, a world of locker rooms minus desire, friendship minus envy, loyalty minus enmeshment. Men were a mystery to me—and thus the objects of my desire. □

During high school Jim's anger toward his father intensified. His dad was well off financially, yet he refused to pay child support or alimony. Jim never saw him; the man never contacted his son. As a result Jim was hungry for male validation: emotionally, spiritually and sexually. By his senior year in high school he had begun to have sex with other men—men who really wanted to be with him.

During high school and college Jim continued going to church, but he was far more interested in his relentless climb toward popularity than any effort he might make into exploring spirituality. In his effort to win friends he went to parties where he found that drinking made him funny—or at least he and his also-drunk teenage friends thought so. In the process he also discovered that both beer and marijuana eased the background pain that lurked in his soul.

Even though Jim was intelligent and outgoing, even though he did well in school, he found himself feeling more and more depressed and angry. Over months and years his drinking increased until during college his depression became so great that he felt he could no longer bear it. Not only was he stoned on marijuana a good portion of the time, but he was often binge drinking on weekends. By then he was rarely attending church services, primarily because he somehow couldn't bear to go. Church bored him and seemed to be full of rules. Worst of all, it brought to his attention another rather disturbing presence: God.

Out of the Closet

While in college Jim announced his homosexuality by coming out to his family and friends. His friends responded by letting him know that his homosexuality was "way cool." Ironically, Jim's popularity soared as he flaunted his newfound sexual identity.

His family, however, felt deeply embarrassed and angry. One brother confronted Jim: "You may not have chosen your sexual orientation, but you have chosen to act on it. I don't think you have a right to be gay when it comes to obeying God."

Jim was livid, but he never forgot his brother's words. Nonetheless, his homosexual behavior continued.

A month later I got seriously involved with Doug, a sensitive ballet dancer. We began dating on Valentine's Day 1982. It felt so right to be romantically involved with a man. Doug and I were both starved for male attention, a codependent's dream come true. We did everything together, even dropping out of college for a semester and touring Europe. Afterward we reentered college and settled down in a nice apartment. Life was lots of fun.

After a year, however, I started to feel suffocated. Who was I? Was I just some projection of this man's ideals? Was I simply living out the expectations of the gay subculture around me? If I was gay, why was I so miserable?

Over time a depression settled into my soul that was as dark and heavy as the grave. Somehow I had left God by the wayside. He had become a distant authority figure. I became upset with his authority. How could God judge me for being gay? Hadn't he made me this way?

I increased my drinking and smoking pot to deal with the depression. I broke up with Doug and entered the gay fast lane: all-night parties plus lots of sex and chemicals. The depression only deepened. I knew it was only a matter of time before I would commit suicide. □

Two years later a wave of despair came crashing over Jim. Late one afternoon he was overwhelmed by tears and deep, agonizing pain. He got into his car and, with tears pouring down his face, drove aimlessly out into the country. He stopped under some trees, looked up at the sky through sun-dappled leaves and spoke to God in angry desperation: "Why have you turned your face away?"

Suddenly the truth hit Jim. God was right there. He always had been. It was Jim who had turned away. In that transforming moment Jim realized what it would cost him to turn back to God. He would have to surrender control of his life. He would have to become God's beloved son. His disciple. His warrior. He would have to be totally God's.

Then another thought struck him deeply: Wasn't that exactly what he had been looking for all along—a Father who loved him? Suddenly the faintest hint of hope stirred within Jim's spirit. Peace began to sift through his soul, like the light filtering down through the leaves above him.

Over the next few months Jim's crushing depression began to lift. That summer God brought an interesting and unique group of friends into his life. He worked with a cast of seven other college students performing musical revues for tourists in West Palm Beach, Florida. Those students changed his life. They and Jim shared an incredible chemistry, both on and off the stage. One of them—a twenty-year-old man named Rod, who was straight— became Jim's closest friend.

Discovering Male Approval

Rod, a fellow performer in the show, was from DePauw University. He had played football in high school. He was a strong, good-looking Midwesterner with a quiet, intense demeanor and a deceptively wry sense of humor. Rod and Jim were friends from day one.

But Jim was shocked. *Why would a straight guy want to hang out with me?* he asked himself. Rod didn't struggle for a second with any attractions to guys in general or Jim in particular. He also knew that Jim had a problem with homosexuality. He didn't care. He liked Jim. He thought Jim was funny. He thought Jim was very talented. And in his nonplussed Midwestern way, he told Jim so.

"You do know you're the leader of the group, don't you?" Rod told Jim.

"What?" Jim had a blank expression on his face.

"You're the leader of the group, Jim. Everybody waits to see what you're going to do, then they do it too because if you do it then they know it's the cool thing to do."

Rod might as well have told Jim "that I was from another planet, or that my insides were made of string cheese. But then, lo and behold, I began to look around and realize, oh my gosh, I *am* the leader of the group. How did that happen? Talk about affirmation."

For Jim that remarkable summer became an exercise in male affirmation and fun. For the first time in his life he began to see himself as a man among men. After the summer ended Jim realized that he wasn't going to bars and hanging out with his gay friends as much as he had before. He also returned to church, established some straight friendships and even dated women.

The struggle, however, wasn't over. Far more than alcohol and drugs, sex had become Jim's coping mechanism for life's harshness. Anytime he felt afraid or disappointed or angry, he had sex. And the more sex he had, the less satisfying it became.

Several years passed without further change. Then, when Jim was twenty-six, his mother made a thought-provoking observation: "When you're finally ready to heal, you'll heal."

Jim knew immediately what she meant: he wasn't experiencing healing because he didn't want it badly enough to give up the habitual sex.

So how did the healing happen? And how does it continue to happen? Well, I had to heal from two things: sexual addiction and the homosexual orientation itself.

Healing of the addiction came via many avenues: small, incremental healings; a journey over time. The most important ingredient though was good Christian counseling, books written by counselors, and friends who had a natural gift for offering good advice. These people and books helped me peel away the romanticism that I had wrapped around my addiction so that I could begin to see it for what it really was.

I remember describing to a counselor a very "romantic" liaison I'd had, how intense it was, how meaningful it felt and so forth.

My counselor shook his head. "That isn't romantic. You basically took a .44 Magnum and shot up your soul."

Because of my relationship with him I was able to receive what he was saying and not push it away. And I began to see my addictive encounters with other men as sad, lonely and gross. This was a real bummer at the time because I was having a lot of liaisons.

What finally woke me up once and for all was a rock-bottom experience that was utterly gross and degrading. I walked away from that encounter saying to myself, "I will never ever put myself in that position again." And I haven't. □

For Jim, healing from the orientation was quite another thing. In his early years of recovery the biggest ingredient in his healing was having Christian male friends with whom he could be honest. They helped him realize that so much of what he had struggled with had nothing to do with gay issues; they were *guy* issues. In other words, all men struggle with their looks, their role, their effectiveness, their self-concept and their confidence.

Finding a Leading Lady

Jim had come to believe that his will had to be totally focused on healing. In fact, if you talk to him today, you'll find that healing has been his focus for fifteen years. He has learned, as he chooses to resist sin, that God empowers his choice. "I can do everything through him who gives me strength" (Philippians 4:13) has become a reality to Jim. And, through God's strength and grace and blessing, Jim has found himself blessed in ways that seemed remote, and even impossible, just a few years ago.

As a performer, Jim travels widely. During one of his tours he met a young woman who worked for a Christian theater company in Houston. He was immediately taken with Carol's magnificent sense of humor. She was pretty and smart and fun. Jim and Carol's first few months of dating were intense and passionate. They were the perfect couple, making beautiful entrances and exits every where they went. But before long the relationship had become a straight reenactment of Jim's relationship with Doug a decade earlier. Soon Jim was once again gasping for emotional breathing space.

He talks about the early days of his relationship with Carol:

Thank goodness for our demented sense of humor. We discovered we could be quite human and quite ungainly with one another. I began to see Carol's ugly side and vice versa, but we decided we still wanted to make the relationship work. I know we both sensed that each other was "the one." But I was struggling with sexual addiction and homosexuality. She was struggling with control and codependency and anger at her father.

Carol had come out of a twelve-year struggle with anorexia and bulimia,

and with God's help she had beaten it. So she knew I could beat sexual addic-
tion, and she hung in there with me as I slipped and slid in our early dating
years. But she had to work through codependency issues. Carol had to learn
that my healing and the success of our relationship were not up to her, that I
wasn't her project. She had to come to the place where, if I didn't pursue heal-
ing, she could let me go. And I had to come to the place that I wasn't pursuing
healing for her but for me. □

Jim and Carol went through a great deal of counseling. They read innumerable books, sat through countless support-group meetings, cried, prayed, ranted and raved. And at the end of it all they somehow continued to love each other. One day Jim realized, "If we can make it through all this and remain in love, we can make it through marriage." That November he asked Carol to marry him. The minute she said yes, they started making wedding plans. Everything seemed wonderful. But underneath it all Jim was terrified.

In January, in a misunderstanding, Carol hurt Jim's feelings. He promptly went to a gay bar and hooked up with a one-night stand. The next day, he told her the truth. After that, the laughter went out of the relationship; a month later they broke up again. Jim went to therapy for sexual addiction. Carol saw a therapist for codependency.

Ironically, that fall they ended up at the same graduate school fifteen hundred miles away and, out of twenty-three thousand students, bumped into each other on the first day. They stayed clear of each other for a while but eventually started dating again. A year and a half later Jim and Carol cautiously got reengaged. After a total of two broken engagements, they were married in 1992. Jim talks frankly about the struggles in their marriage:

It wasn't quite as easy as either of us had imagined. I was twenty-nine.
Carol was thirty-five. Both of us were extremely independent and stubborn.
We had separate bank accounts for the first two years. Though we're both

professional communicators, we had abysmal communication skills one-on-one; we'll probably struggle with that to our graves. But we are also both very tenacious, and once we commit to a path, by golly, that's it.

And on our wedding day, two very tenacious people who truly, deeply love one another tenaciously committed to a life together—and a good one at that. We slowly learned to lean on each other, to be interdependent. We learned to work together, and a national Christian theater ministry called Acts of Renewal has grown out of our marriage. Then we had our first child, a boy, and we learned how much we still had to learn.

It blew our minds, both of us, that suddenly we had to account for our whereabouts 24/7. Carol and I really had to grow up. Then we had another boy. We gave up the selfishness that I don't think either of us thought we could ever do without. Our commitment to our children is so passionate and intense that sometimes I stand amazed at what a good mother Carol is and at how deep my love runs for my two little boys.

Being a parent is a constant source of amazement and delight to me. The love is overwhelming. The responsibility is enormous. The stakes are high. The price is immense. The rewards are extraordinary. To have a little blond-haired, blue-eyed boy look up at you with such love and confidence and trust and say from the bottom of his heart "I love you Daddy" is an experience for which I would (and have) traded all the gay self-actualization in the world. □

Naturally, some of Jim's gay friends assume that he has gone back into the closet. They suspect that he has chosen to suffer in secret agony—the stereotypical gay man who can't live with who he really is. Jim, however, has learned otherwise. He says with a smile that a "gay man" is neither who he is, who he was, nor who he will be.

A Father's Love
Jim believes that the hunger he has had for men is the hunger all humans have—a craving for something to fill the inner emptiness. That hollow ache can never be filled by human relationships, gay,

straight, parental or otherwise. For the Christian, the relationship with God is the love of a lifetime. And it is not some theoretical, spiritualized relationship. It is, rather, an everyday, deep-down dependence and hunger for God that he continues to fill.

Meanwhile, Jim delights in his wife, whom he calls "the second biggest love of my life," after his love for God. They travel together as a husband-and-wife drama team called Acts of Renewal. Both on stage in public and behind closed doors in private, they spar sometimes. They wrestle with issues. At times their communication styles are maddening. But in the midst of it all, Carol and Jim love each other "deeply, grandly, passionately." And they know that God blesses their love.

Is Jim's life free from any pull toward homosexuality? No. The struggle is still there, although much diminished and now understood for what it is—a deception. Despite the temptations, like many others who have left homosexual behavior behind, he has come to know the truth. Following Jesus Christ is the only path that is ultimately fulfilling. All else is an illusion of happiness that eventually leads to death.

The key to freedom for Jim and for so many others is God. God has led him into priceless relationships with friends. God has guided him to books to read. He has brought Jim into situations and encounters that have provided profound healing. Jim believes he is in a process of recovery that God has begun and will finish. "Of course I have to participate in my healing, but it's such a relief to remember that my heavenly dad is a million times more concerned than I am about bringing me into a place of wholeness and Christlikeness."

Jim's concept of God has been changed dramatically over the years. As a boy he viewed God as "a sort of groovy grandparent who loved you and didn't really care what you did." As an adult Christian, Jim read the Old Testament, which deals with God's judgment on his people. This stirred up fear in Jim's heart, and he wasn't able to see how patient God was. He missed the point that, like a good father, God chastises his children, disciplining us so that we will return to him, so that we can experience his love. In recent years Jim has come to know God in a way that has changed his life forever.

The desire of my heart has been to have a father who really wants me. And God has given me that. He's given me himself. So my story isn't over yet. I still have days where the adversary whispers into my mind when I'm tired and disappointed and easily swayed. But I am not his prisoner anymore. I am free to choose life. I'm free to receive the lover of my soul. And I do so daily. ☐

3

A Man of
God's Design

Bill Hernandez

*B*ill Hernandez first realized that he was attracted to other
men as he entered puberty. Oddly enough, this realization wasn't
particularly disturbing to him at first. As a young Hispanic coming
of age in the 1960s, straightening his hair so he could look like the
Beatles was far more important than his sexuality. At least for a
while.

Meanwhile, Bill was receiving sex education at home from his
dad, and it came by example—watching the older man gaze lust-
fully at women and listening to his exaggerated descriptions of the
female body. Later on, when Bill was in his early teens, his dad gave
condoms to his brother and him. "These are for protection," he said
casually. He asked his sons no questions; he gave them no instructions.

Bill describes the father-son relationship like this:

I don't recall a single warm moment with my father. I don't remember him hugging me, kissing me or telling me that he loved me or that I was special. He was just a man who went to work and came home in the evening to eat dinner, watch TV or spend time with his friends. He once said very strongly that there was no such thing as love.

When Dad was around, we children were expected to attend to chores catering to his needs. We removed his shoes and brought him his slippers. We served him food or drinks. We cleaned, mowed the grass, cooked, picked out his gray hair or ironed his clothes. My father once remarked that he had children in order to carry out his whims. My brothers still quote that statement in both disbelief and anger.

My father was very strict, and when I didn't do something, I was either scolded by him, or, in severe situations, he would hit me with his belt or slap me. Sometimes he would become very angry, his face would become livid, and he would hit extra hard. My brother once had welts on his body. Dad was terribly fearsome when he was frustrated. As a result, I remember hiding sometimes when he would come home. I wanted to avoid him. My impression of him was that he was a very demanding person who always got his way. □

Bill's mother, on the other hand, although not especially warm and affectionate, was more relational. She felt she had a special relationship with Bill, and she sometimes told him that she had always wished he'd been a girl. In her family of six sons, Bill was the one she affirmed for his performance in household duties, such as cooking, cleaning, decorating, sewing, shopping, ironing and childcare. Since that was where he got most of his affirmation, he strove to excel in those responsibilities

As for concerns about Bill's dating life, his mother wasn't as interested in his sexual protection as she was about other aspects of male-female relationships. "If you take a girl to the movies," she advised Bill, "she expects you to put your arm around her. If you kiss her, put some muscle into your lips."

Until his father presented him with condoms and his mother began to counsel him about dates, Bill really hadn't given much thought to kissing or any other forms of sexual expression that might follow. The truth was, it had never occurred to him that he was supposed to be aroused when he kissed a girl. He was only mildly concerned about his lack of interest. "Maybe I'm just a late bloomer," he consoled himself.

But there were other complications. During puberty Bill experienced deep bouts of depression during which he cried inconsolably. He was very lonely, while suppressing tremendous anger. As a teenager his family described him as a volcano that occasionally exploded. But that wasn't the most alarming thing his family noticed.

Bill was becoming increasingly effeminate and his parents and brothers frequently pointed it out to him. He was deeply hurt by names like "queer," "faggot," "homo," "sissy" and "pansy," but his family was merciless in trying to correct his effeminate behavior with insults and criticism. In their Hispanic community, with its cultural focus on machismo and sexual posturing, homosexuality was a disgrace. The Hernandez family wanted no part of it.

The more Bill considered his circumstances, the more different he felt. In his search to understand himself, he did some private investigation, searching medical and psychological descriptions in obscure books, which he read secretly in a dark corner of the library. Before long his worst fears were confirmed: Bill was convinced that he was a homosexual.

One day he confessed his discovery to his parents.

Mr. and Mrs. Hernandez were both confused and anxious. Bill's father immediately blamed the boy's mother. "I told you that you should have let me take him to a prostitute!"

"It's not my fault; it's your fault," she retorted angrily.

In his desperate quest for a quick fix, Bill's father took his son to a physician, hoping the doctor would give him a shot to bring Bill's hormones up to par. Instead of prescribing the injections, the doctor recommended that Bill see a psychiatrist. The subsequent counseling did nothing more than enable the young man to become more verbally assertive to his parents. Meanwhile, he continued having homosexual fantasies.

He finally left his family behind when he enrolled in the University of California at Berkeley.

In Search of a New Life

In the fall of 1971 Bill met a young man from Campus Crusade for Christ who introduced him to the Christian gospel. The two met regularly and eventually Bill prayed on his own to accept Jesus as his Lord and Savior. At first he got involved in Bible studies and was very interested in discovering more about the Christian life. But it wasn't long before he began drifting into other activities. And the more involved he got into alcohol and drugs, the more he felt drawn toward homosexual involvement.

One night Bill got very drunk with a college friend. The friend admitted that he was a homosexual.

"I'm bisexual," Bill replied, still unwilling to admit—at least in words—the full truth about himself. But from that night on, Bill slid further and further into homosexuality. He describes the process:

It was mid-1974 when I started going to the bars. I was elated. I couldn't believe there were so many people who thought and felt like me. No one called me names or questioned whether I was normal. Instead people expressed their attraction to me. The gay life seemed to answer my needs for understanding and acceptance. The "real me" was free at last. I shed about forty pounds within a few months, literally dancing the nights away with glee, alcohol, drugs and men.

Right away I found out that I enjoyed affirmation and acceptance more than sex. My first sexual encounter utterly disgusted me. I always had qualms about sex with other men, so I drank or took drugs to rid myself of inhibitions. Still, even after sexual encounters became habitual, deep inside they seemed strange and dirty. □

Bill became a bartender at the White Horse Bar in Oakland, California, a position that made him both popular and available. He got to know many people who frequented the bar and, for Bill, they felt like one big family. In reality, most of the customers were alcoholics and sex addicts looking for a temporary lover. But in his desperate need for acceptance, Bill ignored the negative aspects of gay social life.

"I was in my world, and I couldn't see beyond it," he explains now.

Within a year, however, the joy faded. He had to work harder at attracting other men, and his life became consumed with his desperate search for "Mr. Right." "At times," he says, "my chest literally ached with the pain of loneliness."

Bill continued to inch his way toward alcoholism and drug addiction. Within a year of walking away from his Christian commitment, he was an emotional wreck. One day he found himself sitting on the front steps of St. Mary's Cathedral in San Francisco. As he watched the fog drift by, his eyes filled with tears. He scribbled sadly in his journal: "I really miss my Christian friends. I miss the fellowship and the songs of worship."

Then, just a few days later, it finally happened. "Mr. Right" walked into the bar one night, and Bill promptly forgot any ideas he'd had about leaving homosexuality and returning to Christianity. Bart, his new friend, was different from the other men he'd known. He too wanted a long-term relationship. And unlike so many young gay men in San Francisco, he wasn't just a barhopping "disco queen." Bill explains:

Bart and I lived together for the next two years. Our relationship started out great. We had romantic dinners together, went on long drives and snuggled a lot in front of the TV. But over the following months my desires for love, togetherness and deep communication resulted in something unexpected. I craved the security of that relationship so badly that I compromised my own ideas, aspirations and even my personality to fit the needs of my lover.

I died as a person for the sake of trying to find true love with Bart. We spent time with his friends, but he didn't like mine. I ate the things Bart liked and wore his type of clothes. I began cooking and cleaning, taking the feminine role in our relationship. We lived in a big mansion with a wet bar that had a view of the street. I used to wait there for Bart to come home from work every evening. It wasn't unusual for me to sit there waiting anxiously, tears in my eyes, as darkness fell and dinner got cold.

Over time I drank more alcohol and took more drugs. I became so emotionally unstable that I began to contemplate suicide. My gay relationship was drudgery; work was drudgery; life was drudgery. Everything seemed futile. I had a luxurious apartment, a steady job and a committed lover. I had reached the "top" of the gay world, but I was still lonely and unhappy.

"Lord, pull me out if I get into anything beyond me," I had prayed right before I went into homosexuality. In his love, God was answering my prayer. In my lonely times while living with Bart, I found my old Bible and started reading God's promises again. □

Once he began reading the Bible, the Lord revealed to Bill an objective view of his sexual relationship with Bart. And Bill felt rather foolish. He was able to see that Bart and he had a shallow, twisted imitation of a heterosexual marriage. And in some ways it bore a disturbing resemblance to the relationship between Bill's own parents.

"I no longer want you to be an imitator of your father or mother," the Lord told Bill very clearly. "I want you to be an imitator of me."

Before long, Bill started to rebel in the relationship. Instead of slavishly caring for Bart, he divided all their chores equally. He also started going out on his own.

"Are you seeing someone else?" Bart asked him one day. "You're behaving so differently."

"Yes," Bill informed his startled partner. "I'm having a relationship with Jesus."

Needless to say, Bart thought Bill had gone off the deep end.

Difficult as things had become, making the decision to leave his

lover was not an easy one for Bill. Even though he was convinced
that Jesus really lived and that the homosexuality was wrong, his
emotional life was still deeply entangled with Bart. The prospect of
being lonely again, not to mention living without sex, was almost
more than he could bear. Little by little, even though Bill hung on to
the relationship and continued to live with his lover, the Lord began
convincing Bill that he could meet all of Bill's emotional needs.

Love In Action
In the spring of 1978 Bill heard about an organization called Love
In Action, which ministers to men and women who want to move
away from homosexuality. When he joined their support group, Bill
found people who were very much like he was—they believed in
Jesus Christ and were hoping to leave the gay life behind. They
encouraged him and offered both friendship and prayer support.

After much thought and prayer and conversation, Bill decided to
leave Bart and move into the Love In Action residence program. It
was a huge struggle, and Bill's ambivalence was severe. He left Bart
on April Fool's Day 1978. He shook his head sadly at the irony,
hoping it wasn't a bad omen.

It wasn't. Bill describes those early days at Love In Action:

*In the coming weeks Jesus became real to me in everyday life. He reminded
me of his call on my life: "I want to be your Savior. I want to be your Master.
I want to be your Healer. I want to be your Lover."*

*God answered my prayers in a way that made me feel like he was right
next to me. I prayed about finances and cash came in envelopes and people
provided nice dinners. One time I got lost while driving to someone's house in a
strange town. "Lord, guide me," I prayed. As I turned through several streets,
I landed up right in front of my friend's house.*

*Sometimes while I was praying, I felt hands on me—only to discover that
no one was touching me. One time during a very stressful part of my return to
the Lord I heard fluttering of comforting wings around me. Even though I
couldn't see Jesus, I knew that he was real.*

Jesus took my lover's place. He took my emotional vulnerability and surrounded me with his presence. He urged me to leave the gay lifestyle and, as I stepped out in faith, he met me. □

During the time Bill spent at Love In Action and in subsequent years, he learned many important things about himself. He was able to understand many of the dynamics that contributed to his homosexuality. Most obvious was his relationship with his father. There was no love or warmth in that relationship. The older man was clearly not interested in Bill as a person. And the father's lack of verbal and physical affection simply hadn't prepared the son for healthy relationships of any kind.

Bill's own compliant personality, combined with his father's overbearing one, made a bad situation even worse. Bill didn't have strong opinions to begin with, and his communication skills were almost entirely undeveloped. For a long time he believed that it was unacceptable for him to express his true feelings because it might cause discomfort in others.

Naturally, Bill's homosexual dreams envisioned a lover who was interested in him as a person, who provided him with warmth and affection—the things he needed most from his father. Yet during his homosexual years dominant, controlling men were always more attractive to him. Because his greatest weakness was communicating his needs, wants and feelings, especially with men in authority, Bill often found himself depressed, frustrated and lonely in these relationships.

As his walk with Christ deepened, Bill learned a great deal about forgiveness, and that forgiveness played an important part in his ongoing healing process.

I had to forgive my father for making fun of me with my gay affectations. I also had to forgive him for not being as loving and caring as he could have been. I forgave him for being so overwhelming and manipulative and disrespectful toward me. He emotionally abused me, and I had to come to terms with all the anger I felt toward him. I had to deal with my rejection of him. I remember having great contempt toward him, even hatred. Those were some of the major walls I had to deal with. Later, as I worked through those issues, I began to forgive him for being opinionated, egocentric, narcissistic, bull headed, shaming and proud.

As I forgave the flaws in my father, I discovered that I was indeed very much like him. Finding compassion and mercy for him in these things caused me to accept more compassion and mercy for myself. I also realized that even though there wasn't a lot of outward behavior that showed that I had a bond with my father, inwardly I found that it had been there all along.

The more I made peace with him in my heart, the more I longed to be with him, and our relationship changed dramatically. I could actually say that I loved him. I just could not get enough of my dad. I went fishing with him a few years ago, and he was very patient with me and even baited the hook for me. He accommodated me rather than criticized me. He taught me how to cast the line and praised me often for my aim and form. That day I was the only one who caught a trout. It was a great triumph in many ways.

Most important of all, as I interceded in prayer for my father, he became a Christian. Today most of my family have also become Christians. What a surprise! □

Lessons in Masculinity

The greatest personal issue Bill had to resolve was, in his words, "naming myself a man." After leaving the gay life he saw himself as an "it." Somehow he couldn't come to terms with calling himself a man.

Like many other men who struggle with homosexuality, Bill had defined the word "man" as "experiencing arousal toward women, being able to kid around with the guys, liking sports, having a deep voice, standing head high and chest out, enjoying hunting, getting my hands dirty, knowing auto mechanics, not doing domestic chores and not liking soft colors."

As he interacted with nonhomosexual men, however, he realized his views of being a man were really ill-founded. The most important discovery Bill made was that he was a man simply because God had made him that way. Bill was born male by biological and spiritual design. He could not be anything else at all.

He came to see that theatrical affectation, even though it is often labeled as "gay," does not mean a man is not a man.

He learned that in restrooms many normal men make a dash for a private stall rather than the urinal. He heard them complain that they wouldn't be caught dead standing at a urinal unless they were alone because they were modest. Modesty, he found out, is not homosexual.

He came to see that many straight males are sexually disinterested in women from time to time. Sexual disinterest or dysfunction is not homosexual.

Bill found out, from both straight and ex-gay men, that having passing homosexual feelings is not homosexual. Acting on those feelings is.

Regarding stereotypical "gay" behavior, Bill explains:

I've worked on not having a high-pitched voice and ridding myself of various affected postures such as no crossing of ankles, no gliding across the floor with a straight back, no hand on hip, no covering of mouth in astonishment and no rotating of my shoulders like Joan Crawford when I walk. When I speak in public, I rehearse and tell myself that I'm not Marilyn Monroe with a breathy voice, and I try not to roll my eyes. That doesn't communicate who I truly am.

I got a special gift of healing one day when I went to a plant nursery and asked this guy there about growing bulbs. I was secretly growing bulbs on my deck, terrified that I might be gender and mentally diseased. It's true—I'm not exaggerating. With great scientific interest and detail about soil, nutrients and lighting the nurseryman helped me with my gardening interests. I couldn't help but notice that he had a football player's build and seemed heterosexual to the core.

I realized as he talked to me that growing a flower or not knowing the sports scores didn't make me a homosexual. Doing homosexual acts made me homosexual. That nursery experience had a profound impact on how I saw myself. God has continued to use small, everyday things to help me with my self-image. By the way, my bulbs are not color coordinated, just colorful and a miracle of creation as they emerge.

When I began to see that normal men could exhibit a host of behaviors and affinities, I realized that I had been lied to about what a man was. My biology and spiritual design transcends any cultural behavioral expectations. That has been a great healing for me because I have learned to love myself as a unique male, and that pleases God. I now respect what God has created. I now tell every homosexually inclined person I talk to that they are "developmentally deficient heterosexuals," and most of them find that a great relief. □

Reparenting with the Heavenly Father

Bill has learned, as so many who struggle with homosexuality have discovered, that God is the loving, tenderhearted parent that so many of us have lacked. And as we struggle to understand our relationship with our earthly parents, to understand the toll those relationships have taken in our lives and the need for forgiveness, we have a powerful alternative available to us. In John 3:16 we read, "God so loved the world that he gave his one and only Son, that whoever believes in him shall not perish but have eternal life."

God our heavenly Father initiated salvation and healing. He did what no earthly father could do. The Lord took the initiative to find each of us and to guide us into wholeness. As Bill points out:

My earthly father did what he felt was best, which had its shortcomings, but my heavenly Father has exercised perfect love in working with me. He has become my true father. My return to him involved him intervening in miraculous ways, visions and illumination of Scripture. As a result, I have become emotionally dependent on him. I have found him to be a parent who cares for even the smallest details in my life. I can't say I reparented myself or allowed God to be my true father. He initiated the whole process, and I simply responded with the help of the Holy Spirit within me. □

For Bill, being reparented by God did not happen alone, in a prayer closet. It happened in relationship with other people whom God sent Bill's way. Reparenting was demonstrated through the unconditional love, warmth, encouragement and discipline of God's people. Their generosity, patience and prayers helped him to grow up. "I could see parenting gifts from the Lord coming through other people from whatever age, race or color. I inherited a new personality in Jesus. If we open up to him, he opens the world to us."

Bill has been out of homosexual activities for over twenty-two years. Today he serves on pastoral staff at a church in San Francisco. Nothing has been more critical to his new life than his relationship with Jesus Christ. He has focused on knowing God, and healing has followed in all areas of his life. He reports with great joy that over the years his homosexual feelings have faded to a whisper, while heterosexual feelings have emerged more and more. His new desires and feelings are a daily reminder that God's presence restores us in profound ways. Heterosexuality was never his goal, he'll be quick to tell you. But he also realizes that it is a welcome byproduct of his fascination with the Lord. Bill concludes:

As exciting as personal restoration is, nothing is more wonderful or as interesting as Jesus. He's the center of my life now. I'm emotionally dependent on him. He's as fresh as when I first encountered him. My favorite Scripture is in Hebrews 13:5, 8: "Never will I leave you; never will I forsake you. . . . Jesus Christ is the same yesterday and today and forever." His promises are true. God has been faithful. I'm no longer lonely because God has healed me through the rich fellowship of his presence. □

4

A Hopeless Verdict Overturned

Jane Boyer

*Y*ou're gay and there's nothing you can do about it!"

These words, spat out at Jane Boyer by one of her lovers, resounded in her ears with a terrible finality. No matter how deeply she wanted to be a devoted wife, a loyal Christian and a good mother, the words sounded like truth. In fact, it seemed to Jane that everything that had happened in her life up until that very conversation confirmed the hopelessness of her lover's verdict.

Jane was the victim of an alcoholic family. Her violent father had abused her. She had been sexually molested during her childhood. From her earliest years she had experienced same-sex attractions. And for as long as she could remember, Jane had loathed men.

The die seemed to have been cast. And yet Jane has beaten the odds. Today she is a joyful feminine woman and a powerful speaker who is sought after in many places for her testimony of overcoming lesbianism. She and her husband have a fulfilling marriage, which at one time seemed doomed to certain failure. How did these incredible changes occur?

A Catholic Upbringing

Jane's parents were French Catholic. Occasionally the family attended Sunday mass or dressed up to celebrate midnight mass on Christmas Eve. But hers was not really a Christian household. Alcohol, not a lively Christian faith, was the focal point of the family's activities. Violence was not uncommon in their daily life. Yet in spite of everything, as Jane describes it, she was an exceptionally spiritual child.

I attended a very small Catholic school from kindergarten through seventh grade. I developed strong emotional attachments with the nuns, and though these relationships were very enmeshed, they provided security for me in the midst of a very violent and abusive environment at home.

By age five I had a strong curiosity regarding the saints, the Virgin Mary and the martyrs. Most of all, I had a deep faith in Jesus and hoped to serve him, much like the saints I'd read about. □

Light Versus Darkness

Sadly, during Jane's teenage years her bright spiritual nature, her longing and devotion were eclipsed by dark, earthbound realities. First of all, both Jane and her mother suffered physical abuse during Jane's father's alcoholic rages. Their home life was always off-balance and unpredictable. The only certainty was that before long, the rage would erupt, and they would find themselves, once again, in harm's way.

During this time Jane formed two very strong opinions. First of all, she developed an intense hatred for men. Her father represented to her the worst aspects of the "stronger" sex, and she wanted nothing to do with any male, primarily because of his excessive behavior.

Second, because her mother was a victim of her father's violence,

Jane became the older woman's protector and caretaker. "Mom," she screamed at her mother on more than one occasion, "I hate it that you are weak, clingy and powerless. I will not be like you. I want nothing to do with womanhood!"

Still the worst was yet to come. Jane was not only molested, she also faced what must have seemed like an endless battle against sexual predators. Her first abuse took place when she was about eight years old, perpetrated by a troubled teenage boy who had moved in with their family on a temporary basis.

Another incident followed, involving a neighbor—an older man whom Jane can barely recall. Fortunately or not, the details are lost to her. But she hasn't forgotten everything. She describes some of the males who surrounded her in those troubled childhood years:

> *Two of my uncles made me very uncomfortable. Their comments and the way they looked at me felt sexual in nature. Meanwhile, I worked at our family gas station and was occasionally sexually exploited by male customers. And, of course, my father frequently made degrading remarks, often sexual ones, regarding women in general and specifically regarding my body.*
>
> *Meanwhile, as far back as I can remember, I felt intense emotional attractions toward women, primarily my teachers. I craved their attention, and I never seemed to get enough of it. I couldn't help but notice that my peers were not going through this sort of emotional experience. Consequently, I was ashamed and embarrassed. "Jane, you are different," I told myself again and again. "You are weird."* □

As if she hadn't struggled enough, or perhaps because of the stress she continuously endured, Jane's face was ravaged by the inner turmoil she faced every day. She suffered from severe acne. But that wasn't the only thing. It seemed to her that in every way her physical appearance was a continually painful problem. She was a late bloomer in her physical development, a fact that caused her tremendous shame and forced her to encounter an inordinate amount of teasing.

"Overall," Jane recalls, "I felt extremely ugly. In response, I developed a rebellious attitude and began drinking alcohol and doing drugs to numb the inner pain."

A Husband and a Gay Bar

High school came and went, and, when Jane turned eighteen, she joined the U.S. Army. During her tour of duty, while she was stationed in San Francisco, she met Mike Boyer. Despite her distaste for men and all they had represented in her life, she married him. Together the two of them drank and did drugs, partied and made their way across the country. They continued this dissolute lifestyle for a few years.

Finally, in 1980 Mike and Jane settled in Maine. Although she had continued to experience same-sex attractions throughout the early years of her marriage, it was in Maine that Jane first went to a gay bar. The exciting, highly charged homosexual scene she discovered there became her secret addiction for the next five years. A double life had begun.

Jane drank heavily, used drugs and involved herself in wild sexual acts on Saturday nights. On Sunday mornings she went to church, where she cried, grieved and repented. Unfortunately, her repentance wasn't enough to help her overcome her desperate need for female attention and affection. "I became very popular in the gay community," Jane recounts.

I was even awarded the runner-up award in the local Ms. Lesbian Popularity contest. I was involved in a Christ-centered church, but it was so large I could easily hide out. My first relationship was on and off for about four years, the second relationship lasted about a year.

Was I born homosexual? *I wondered.*

A therapist counseled me, "Your problem is your inability to accept who you really are."

I couldn't help but take her words seriously. I began to believe there was no hope for change and no future for my marriage. □

In the mid-1980s Jane spilled out her story to her pastor. She revealed to him both her struggle with lesbianism and her hatred of men. The pastor clearly didn't know what to do. He was quite unprepared for her confession. But, despite his inexperience, he said something very important. "Jane, you might leave Mike and pursue the gay life," he told her. "And God will still always love you. But you will never be blessed."

That's basically all her pastor said. But, for some reason, Jane could not forget his words.

Over the course of the next few years Jane did make a decision to deal with her drinking problem. And once she had put her alcohol dependency behind her, she told Mike that she wanted him to leave for a while because of his own drinking problem. He agreed to a temporary separation. Her husband traveled west, which bought some time for Jane to figure out what she wanted to do. She wrestled with her options, but the battle was short-lived. Within days her lover moved in with her and her two children.

Things weren't perfect between the two women, but they continued their relationship in relative harmony. One day on the kitchen table her lover left a love note to Jane. That same day Mike returned to the house earlier than expected. He walked in and looked around to see what was going on.

His eyes rested on the note.

Mike literally fell to his knees, crying out, "God, you've got to help me. Look what's happened to my marriage! I need you to step in and do something about this!"

The Lord immediately confronted Mike: "How can I heal your marriage if you won't give up the booze?"

Mike never drank again. Jane recalls that tumultuous day when her world also came crashing down around her.

Within the hour Mike called me at the office. "Jane, you need to make up your mind. You can't go on living like this. But let me warn you. If you decide to live the gay life, I will not allow our children to be raised in that kind of environment."

I knew that he was right. I was faced with making the most difficult decision of my life: choosing between the man I married—for whom I had no desire—and the woman whom I felt I could not live without. I had to choose between the gay community where I felt support and acceptance, and the church—which seemed so cold and detached.

I was in the deepest despair. The conflict was unbearable. I contemplated suicide.

"Lord Jesus," I cried, "I have made a mess of my life. Please help me!"

The very next day Mike visited a Bible bookstore and found a book about gays who had changed. Perhaps because I had come to a place of such hopelessness, feeling that there was nowhere to turn, I read every word in one sitting. That book restored my hope. And it was through the book that I found out about Exodus. □

A month later, in June 1989, Jane left her husband, children and lesbian lover back in Maine and drove to Pennsylvania to attend her first Exodus conference. As she headed south across New England, she asked herself the same questions again and again: *Will I find the answers I'm looking for? Is it true that homosexuals can change? Is there really hope for me?*

"And That Is What Some of You Were"

The conference caught Jane off guard; its atmosphere and message took her by surprise. During the praise and worship times she witnessed love for Jesus and a sincerity and openness that she'd never seen before. There was nothing cold and detached about this group of Christians. The so-called former homosexuals seemed to know to the depths of their being the reality of God's forgiveness. And they certainly understood what it meant to worship him.

As a five-year-old girl Jane had begun a relationship with God. Now at the Exodus conference, decades later, something new and powerful began to well up inside her. She somehow began to believe that, in spite of everything that had happened to her, she could experience genuine intimacy with Jesus.

At the same time, God had not forgotten Jane's search for answers, and she also learned the truth about homosexuality. She had heard the apostle Paul's statement before that those involved in homosexuality "would not inherit the kingdom of God." But for the first time Jane learned at the Exodus conference that Paul had followed that statement with another, which was completely amazing to her:

"And that is what some of you were" (1 Corinthians 6:9-11).

"Some of you *were*." Past tense. Paul might as well have said, "But that's not what you are any more!" Hope surged within Jane. Yes, change was possible. It no longer mattered what secular "research" revealed. Jesus had clearly said that Jane could be set free!

There was more to learn—much more. Jane explains:

I came to realize that we perceive God based on the kinds of relationships we've had as children. Men had violated me physically, emotionally and sexually. Therefore, I assumed that God, who reveals himself as masculine, could not be trusted.

During the conference Jesus said to me, "I can heal those hurts, but you have to give up your lesbian relationship."

I panicked. "But Lord, you don't understand! It's the best love I've ever known, and I don't want to give it up."

Despite my fears, God was calling me to a radical obedience. With an act of my will I made the decision to end the lesbian relationship. Still I wondered, "Can God fill this emptiness within me, this longing to be loved?"

During a prayer time at the conference, with the "eyes of my heart," I saw a picture. I was three years old, standing a few feet away from Jesus. His arms were outstretched, his eyes radiated love. Then he picked me up and held me. At that moment the love of Jesus came pouring into my heart, filling it up to overflowing.

I realized right then and there that lesbian love was a counterfeit. It had never filled and never satisfied the deepest needs of my heart. But now I had found Jesus. He was a man I could trust, someone whose love truly fills and satisfies.

I didn't hesitate. At last I knew the truth. In my heart I closed the door once and for all to homosexuality. I struggled for awhile, but I never looked back. □

When she returned home, Mike couldn't believe the change he saw in Jane's face. "What on earth has happened to you?" he asked, half-afraid to hear what she had to say.

"I have fallen in love with another man," Jane smiled, "and his name is Jesus. And I've found out the truth about lesbianism."

Sensing that his prayers were finally being answered, Mike was more than excited. Could it be true that, at last, there was a future for their marriage? Did he dare get his hopes up?

New Life, Renewed Love

Jane couldn't have been more serious about her decision to leave homosexuality behind. She broke off the lesbian relationship, never returned to the gay bar and avoided her gay friends. For a while it was tough being cut off from her emotional lifeline. She quickly realized that giving up the sexual part was easy compared to the agony of working through the emotional dependence she had developed with her former lover. It took months to grieve the loss of that relationship.

Meanwhile, it took several years for Mike to work through his anger at having been betrayed and to begin trusting Jane again. She describes the rebuilding of their deeply scarred relationship:

Only through Jesus Christ were we able to love again. He gave my husband the grace to forgive me and to understand the roots underlying my lesbianism. Mike also had the patience to stand with me as I worked through my brokenness and my sexual, emotional and physical abuse issues, along with addressing my anger and fears toward men.

Through hard work and a relationship with Jesus to carry us through, my husband and I enjoy a close relationship today. Healing from sexual brokenness has been an ongoing process—developing deeper intimacy with Christ and learning to be vulnerable with Mike as well as with others. □

Jane's children had been very young during much of her struggle. Fortunately they were not able to understand the nature or
details of her particular problem, although the strain on the marriage during that time was certainly obvious. Since then homosexuality has become a household word to Mike and Jane's children
because they have been exposed to their mother's testimony time
and again. The children are now teenagers and have a unique
understanding of the root causes of homosexuality. As a result, they
too are compassionate toward those who struggle.

Jane continues to thank God for that first Exodus conference she
attended and for the powerful way he used it to change her life, to save
her marriage and to get her back on track with him. "I will always be
grateful to God for his work of restoration in my life," she says.

*My husband and I are quite involved in the lives of our two teenagers. I am
near completion of my graduate studies and will be employed full-time as a
nurse practitioner in the field of chemical dependency and counseling, specifically dealing with those who have experienced childhood trauma. I have close
female friendships today without dependence, eroticization or enmeshment. By
the grace of God, I no longer struggle with lesbian desires.*

*I work with Focus on the Family in speaking around the country about
homosexuality. My children have recently expressed an interest in accompa-
nying me to some of those conferences.*

*To those who struggle with homosexual behavior, same-sex attractions or
gender confusion, I offer this advice: Develop a strong relationship with Jesus
Christ. Practice radical obedience to his Word. With an act of your will, close
the door once and for all to homosexual behavior, and the healing process will
begin.*

*However, we have to remember that our primary goal must not be healing
from homosexuality. Our goal—whatever our struggle, whatever our need—
is to develop an intimate relationship with the Lord Jesus Christ.* □

5

"The Best News
I've Ever Heard!"

Jason Thompson

I was fourteen and sitting alone in my grandparents' house with a Bible on my lap. Since my father was an Episcopal minister and I had been raised in a Christian home, I was familiar with many Bible stories. But that day I desperately needed to know what God had to say about homosexuality. After reading for a while, it was abundantly clear from his Word that God considered homosexuality a sin (Leviticus 18:22; Romans 1:26). This discovery made me more confused than ever. □

So begins Jason Thompson's story about his struggle with homosexual feelings. As a young teenager Jason was desperately caught between the "normal" way of life he saw all around him, the proper male-female relationships he saw at his church, and the deep and relentless stirrings within himself.

Not long before his biblical search for answers, Jason had a vivid and powerful dream in which he found himself engaging in homosexual behavior. He awakened with a start, feeling both scared and confused. From that time on, Jason felt an increasing desire to be close physically to his male peers.

Where were the desires coming from? Jason asked himself the same questions again and again, hating the feelings that continued to tease and torment him. He had no idea what was stirring up the cravings, but he knew to the core of his being that he didn't want them. He was also determined to keep his strange feelings a secret. As he wrestled with homosexual desire, Jason prayed earnestly for God to take it all away. Unfortunately, the feelings didn't disappear.

"Why isn't he answering my prayers?" Jason questioned. He wondered if God really even cared.

Predictably high school brought further confusion. Unsure of his sexual identity Jason sought out male friends with whom he could experience emotional closeness, all the while wishing and hoping for physical intimacy. An episode of sexual experimentation with one of his friends took place one night. The experience satisfied some of the curiosity that had been created by his fantasy life, but he wasn't at all satisfied. No matter how fervently he continued to pray about his struggles, God still did not take away his same-sex desires.

As a senior Jason finally gathered up enough courage to reach out for help. He located the phone number of a teen counseling help line. After he nervously spilled out his story to the woman who took the call, she coldly replied, "The guy who deals with the gays will be in on Friday."

Jason was humiliated. He says:

I threw the phone down in frustration and climbed on my red Honda Elite scooter. Speeding through the side streets of southeast Portland, I felt angry and hopeless; I even thought about killing myself by slamming into a parked car. But God stopped me from acting on that thought and calmed my heart. □

By the fall of 1990 Jason had found a girlfriend at church. They started to date and Jason pretended to be interested in her, but the strain of his conflicted feelings grew apparent to those who knew him. Finally, to his own amazement, in a frightening conversation Jason confided his homosexual struggle to this young woman.

Surprisingly, she had words of hope and encouragement for Jason. She even tracked down the phone number of The Portland Fellowship, a local Exodus ministry. Jason picked up the phone and placed the call.

Phil Hobizal, director of The Portland Fellowship, listened attentively to Jason's story. Rather than passing him on to someone else, or rejecting him because of his homosexual feelings, Phil assured Jason that help was available. The two of them arranged to meet the following week.

"Change is possible," Phil confidently encouraged Jason.

"That's the best news I've ever heard!" Jason replied.

A Flawed Relationship with Dad

Jason wanted his parents to know about his struggle but was convinced that he couldn't talk to his dad about it. He had always felt distant and detached from him. While he had frequently shared his thoughts and feelings with his mother, he had never felt as if he had that kind of freedom with his dad. He describes their relationship:

While growing up it didn't seem out of the ordinary. It wasn't strange. It's just the way my father was. I didn't have any animosity or resentment toward him. In terms of correction, in a sense he was a very passive father. He didn't spank me, discipline me or ground me. In our family all that was really my mom's responsibility. So I didn't have any fear of my dad.

But at the same time I don't think I had any real closeness with him, either. I wasn't always waiting for Dad to get home so we could play or do something together. He just wasn't what I would consider a playmate or someone I wanted to spend time with. And the pressures of ministry kept him away from home a lot of evenings.

Since my dad was a minister in the church, I looked up to him, knowing that he was a man of God and that he cared for people. So in a lot of ways I respected my dad. I didn't want to harm him, nor did I want to badmouth him. A couple of times I actually felt really close to him, but there were very, very few times like that. He was responsible and always did everything he could to provide money for the household and to put food on the table. But when it came to relational or personal issues, Dad wasn't really someone that I could connect with.

I remember on one occasion walking to church with my dad and feeling like we were having a really good conversation—a conversation that just meant so much to me. We were talking about life and nothing in particular. Later my mom asked, "How was your time with Dad?"

"Oh, we had such a heart-to-heart conversation, kind of a man-to-man conversation."

And my dad looked at me with a really puzzled look on his face, as if to say, "What do you mean? We didn't have any man-to-man talk."

In retrospect I think he thought I meant that we'd had a conversation about sex, the kind of things men talk to men about. But my perception of our "connection," our father-son moment, got shattered because it was not what he thought; it wasn't what he saw. □

On the other hand, Jason's mother was the kind of person with whom he could share deep thoughts and spend quality time. He still remembers when she would come into his room first thing in the morning, wake him up and then sit at the foot of his bed and talk to him about life. She had a true interest in Jason, and he felt genuinely connected to her. When she was down and hurting, he felt empathetic, and he often felt as if he needed to be there for her, to encourage and build her up. For one thing, the Thompsons were not financially secure. They had even lived for a couple of years in a renovated bus. It wasn't a particularly negative experience for Jason, but it was doubtless a difficult time for his parents.

Although he had grown up in his father's Episcopalian congregation, during his teenage years, Jason became involved with a charismatic church. His personal search for God had led him in a different denominational direction from his family. And now he wondered if this homosexual problem would drive him even further away.

Nevertheless, a few days after contacting The Portland Fellowship Jason decided to take the risk and approached his mother tentatively. "There's something I need to talk to you about. I . . . I've been struggling with homosexual tendencies, but . . ."

She stopped Jason short before he could finish his confession. "Wait. Let me get your father. He needs to hear this too."

"No, wait Mom. I don't think he'll understand."

"It's important, Jason. He needs to know," she insisted.

Jason's fear and nervousness soared. There was no way out of the ensuing discussion. He paced the house while his mother went outside and called his dad.

Once Rev. Thompson was settled in the room, Jason took a deep breath and explained his situation. "I have been struggling," he began, "with homosexuality."

After giving them a brief description of his difficulties, Jason also told them about the hope he had gained from The Portland Fellowship. His father and mother listened politely. They did not judge him or condemn him. Once all had been said and done, Jason left his parents' house feeling a freedom that he had never before experienced. The weight of the secret he had kept for years began to evaporate. Later he found out that his parents were awake most of that night talking, crying and praying.

The next Sunday Jason went to his father's church. Before the service his dad spoke with him outside. "Jason," he said, "I've seen many people with serious problems during my years of ministry, but I have never seen anyone deal with a problem so diligently as you. I've never been as proud of you as I am today."

No Quick Fix

Blessed as he was by his parents' love and supportive words, Jason's first year of involvement at The Portland Fellowship was difficult. During the group's Tuesday night meetings he learned about the roots of his homosexual desires. He was introduced to God's plan of forgiveness and was given tools that could help him forge the freedom that he so deeply desired from his homosexual struggle. But there was no quick fix for his feelings.

Occasionally on weekends Jason would ride into downtown Portland on his scooter. Most of the time he was "just looking," checking out what was available in the gay community, secretly cherishing the hope that someone or something could fill the still-gaping pit of emotional need inside him.

Pornography still had a powerful hold on his life, and it was proving to be a barrier to his relationship with God. Finally, after a full year of participation with The Portland Fellowship, Jason realized that he could not have it both ways: he couldn't follow God and yet continue to nurture the hope of satisfying his homosexual urges. He describes the way he felt reined in by God.

I had a hunger for promiscuity. I had such a desire to go out and engage sexually with anonymous people. I knew a lot about the anonymous arena. I knew about the parks and the bookstores. But God wouldn't let me go to those places. He kept me out of trouble through my fear of being caught, my fear of getting AIDS, and my sense of feeling gross about the whole thing.

A couple of times I engaged in anonymous behavior, but I did nothing that would allow me to contract AIDS. It wasn't full-blown homosexual behavior, it was more visual stimulation and mutual touch. And immediately after experiences like that I'd feel devastated. Sometimes I even thought about suicide because I knew how awful and wrong those things were. Promiscuity was never a big thing with me. My sin was more in my mind, my fantasies, my thoughts, my desires. □

Like so many boys and men who struggle with homosexuality, the biggest lesson Jason had to learn was that he suffered from a lack of affirmation and bonding from the same sex, a lack that inevitably led back to his relationship with his father. Considering his dad's personality, it wasn't difficult to put the puzzle together. His father was not absent, uncaring or irresponsible. The older man simply had a difficult time knowing what a father was and how to relate, how to communicate, how to be vulnerable—all those kind of things. And Jason, with his sensitive nature, had a greater need than a man with his father's personality could fill.

In a similar way, Jason found that the male body was a curiosity to him, primarily because he had never seen his father or brother naked. Because of his desire to know what other males looked like, he became fascinated by pornography.

Another root element in Jason's struggle with homosexuality was the peer rejection he had suffered as a young boy. He had been overweight as a child and was insultingly labeled by other children. This rejection caused him to be isolated and to spend an inordinate amount of time in fantasy where he withdrew to protect himself.

I would admit different people in my head, not sexually, but as models of what I wanted to be. When I was about eight years old, one of them was Superman. I definitely longed to be a person like that—someone who was looked up to, someone who was powerful and strong. Superman represented every characteristic that I was lacking or that I didn't see in my father or brother or other male figures in my life. And so I hungered for that.

I was so driven to find masculinity. I didn't act out sexually because I didn't have any connections. But because I was so fantasy prone in the first place due to the Superman thoughts and other desires, it was easy for me to take a male image and sexualize it. Then the onslaught of sexual feelings at puberty and being able to have an orgasm and all those kind of things tied in together. Sexual fantasy came to be a very powerful experience for me. □

So it was in his late teens that Jason found himself crying out to God to overcome his same-sex longings. He desperately wanted God to take away the feelings. But Jason learned that God didn't want to take anything away from him. Instead he wanted to give Jason something: healing, hope and wholesomeness. God wanted to give Jason new friends, a new identity, a new understanding of masculinity, a new way to think about men and new ways to have relationships with women. God couldn't just take away the hunger without meeting Jason's real needs. Today Jason says, "That was one of the most powerful things I learned in the process of healing in my life."

Men who seek to change their homosexual orientation often have to deal with behaviors and mannerisms that identify them as gay. Jason never developed those mannerisms and behaviors. In fact, there were those who thought that Jason was a football player or an athlete, even though he had no such inclinations.

Over the course of his school years he was labeled as "fatso" and "loner," but he was never accused of being a homosexual. He never felt like a girl or felt overly connected to girls. Nor did he hang out with people who were effeminate, so no one ever accused him of such things. His struggle was internal, secret and agonizing.

While he was attending Bible college, Jason lived in the dorm and shared his struggle with some of his male friends. It was a terrifying risk, and although not everyone knew quite how to handle this issue, Jason didn't experience rejection. In fact, one of the first young men with whom he shared became one of his closest friends. He reports:

God was answering my prayers. His desire was not just to take away all my problems but to provide the body of Christ to come alongside to support and encourage me. It was through being open and sharing my struggle with others that I began to have my real needs fulfilled.

I became a small-group leader at The Portland Fellowship and continued to walk in submission to God. I could see that intense emotional needs for male friendship were driving my desires. But slowly, through positive male friendships, my homosexual desires began to fade away.

One of the greatest steps I made in the change process began one night during a long conversation with my dad. We set up a time where just he and I could go out to dinner and talk—straight from our hearts. For the first time we shared with each other the most personal things in our lives. I felt a new connection to him, one that began to take away some doubt and uncertainty about our relationship. □

In January 1993 Jason joined the staff of The Portland Fellowship because he wanted the opportunity to tell people that change is possible. He longed to reach teenagers with the good news of freedom from a life dominated by sexual sin. Over the next few years he matured spiritually, working in ministry and attending classes to complete his degree in biblical studies.

The Right Girl at the Right Time

But during this time of growth Jason wrestled with yet another concern. He felt no attraction at all toward women. At times he was able to see that a girl was attractive outwardly—she might look pretty, but for him even that was a nonissue. His full energy and desire was toward good-looking guys because he wanted to be like them; he wanted to embrace them; he wanted them to accept him. Then and only then, he felt somewhere in his heart, would he have worth, would he feel good about himself, would he somehow achieve masculinity.

As he wrestled with these issues, Jason deeply longed to have romantic and sexual desires for women. Sometimes he would even try to force those desires by thinking of some specific woman and trying to sexualize her. Predictably, such imaginings left him feeling both empty and dishonest. Eventually he gave up. He stopped trying to fantasize about women and just rested in the sort of asexual place he inhabited. He was no longer sexualizing men, but he didn't really want women either.

At times I cried out to God in anguish and in tears. On lonely Friday nights, especially, I longed to start dating and to ask somebody out for the first time. As I prayed, I promised God that I would never ever ask a girl out until I was honestly attracted to her in some way. I would not play games with a woman. I would not use her to see if I was interested. It had to be an initial attraction and then a real honest desire to ask her out on a date because I wanted to get to know her. That internal desire had to come from God. It couldn't be something I created. It couldn't be something I faked. And so I just waited for that attraction to come.

One day while hanging out with some friends at the college coffee shop, I looked across the table and noticed a beautiful young woman. Her smile and friendly nature attracted my attention. □

Jason's first response to Amy was an answer to his deepest prayers. He was immediately aware of a different feeling, a different response to this young woman. Something about her captured his attention. She seemed fun. She was attractive. She was somebody he really wanted to get to know, to ask out on a date.

Jason suddenly faced another unique dilemma. That day in the coffee shop he sat there thinking. "How do I do this? Do I write her a note? One of those notes in junior high where it says, 'Will you go out with me? Check box: Yes. No. Or maybe.' I had no idea how to do it."

Fortunately Jason moved beyond his momentary fears, summoned his courage and asked Amy out on a date. They enjoyed the evening, and during the following months he found his affection for her growing deeper as they spent more time together. Jason faced each fear as it arose and felt amply rewarded as his confidence in their relationship grew.

Amy became my first real girlfriend. She knew little about homosexuality, but because of her desire to know me better and learn what I did, she participated in the eight-month Portland Fellowship program that includes teachings on the root causes of homosexuality and how Christ could help us find freedom.

Exactly a year after our first date I took her to Multnomah Falls—a famous local spot where my dad had proposed to my mom. I dropped down on one knee and asked Amy to be my wife. She was so startled that I almost dropped her ring over the bridge near the falls! Thankfully, she said yes.

Our wedding on March 15, 1997, was a beautiful ceremony with our friends and loved ones right by our sides and supporting us all the way. We entered marriage with an incredible honeymoon in Puerto Vallarta, Mexico, and have been enjoying marriage ever since. □

Like many ex-gays, however, Jason found that marriage was not a magic solution to escaping all of life's pressures and challenges. After three and a half years of marriage, Jason and Amy had a baby daughter, Abigail, who was born with severe heart defects. They knew of her health problems long before she was born and were told that she would either require a heart transplant or the Norwood procedure (a three-stage heart operation). The Thompsons lived with increasing bouts of anxiety as the birth date approached. Jason recalls what Abbie's early days were like:

The first week of her life was a roller-coaster ride. Five minutes after she was born, the doctor informed us that, because of a weakened right ventricle, the heart transplant became our only option. Over the weekend God changed that. He healed the weak area, and the Norwood was back on.

The operation went well, but that night we were called to her side because the doctors didn't think she would make it through the night. But God changed that too. Amy and I stepped out in the hall by the elevator for a good cry, and when we stepped back in, her vital signs were stable. □

The recovery process was much longer than expected, but Jason and Amy rejoiced each day that tiny Abigail survived. After a month of living in the hospital, they were finally allowed to take their little girl home. Due to Abigail's complex medical needs, care was necessary almost around the clock, and many people from the Thompsons' church helped with shopping, laundry, cooking, cleaning and a host of other chores.

After three and a half months, Jason and Amy received their doctor's permission to take an out-of-town trip with their infant daughter. However, after they had driven several hours from home, Abigail began showing symptoms of respiratory distress. Jason and Amy sped to the nearest hospital, but Abigail's condition worsened. Her tiny heart stopped beating, and she was revived and then airlifted to a larger hospital. But her heart stopped again, and resuscitation attempts failed. On that Sunday night, February 4, 2001, Jason and Amy were faced with one of the most heart-breaking situations any parents can face: the death of their child.

In the days that followed, the Thompsons received an outpouring of love and support from their church family and ministry friends around the country. Their church was filled with friends from near and far for Abigail's memorial service. "This little girl touched so many people's lives—and she never spoke a word," said one elder to the several hundred people who gathered to remember Abigail. The Thompsons knew they would always miss Abigail, but they were comforted to know that they would see her again someday in heaven.

In the past year Jason has been forced to grow immensely in his role as husband and father. In the midst of the challenges he realizes that he has learned many positive things from his own father—a love for people, a love for ministry and years of hard-won wisdom—which he prays he can combine with the affection and attention he wasn't always able to experience.

Today, Jason is codirector of The Portland Fellowship; he has also recently been appointed director of Exodus Youth, a new outreach to teens who are struggling with sexual identity issues. Jason and Amy are fellowship leaders for a young married group in their church, and Jason has been ordained as a minister of the gospel. His pastors ordained him on the weekend of his wedding.

Jason believes with all his heart that freedom is available to those who struggle with homosexuality—genuine freedom and not what he describes as "white-knuckling it." Jason believes in the kind of freedom that means not having to say no every day to homosexual thoughts and feelings. He affirms that as we walk with God we are able to experience a genuine renewing of our minds, enabling us to overcome whatever temptations may assault us.

He rejoices in the realization that today, when he is in the presence of other males, he no longer has feelings of either sexual or emotional desire for them. Instead there is inner confidence. There is the ability to look at men and say, "I feel like one of them. I *am* one of them. They are just like me. They have struggles just like I do. We are alike."

At the same time, Jason is able to enjoy Amy relationally, emotionally, sexually and spiritually. "I love my wife," he says. "I am so at peace with who I am with her and the joy that she brings me in life. I am never wishing, never wanting to return to who I was before—feeling that craving and that hunger for men to come alongside and embrace me and love me and accept me."

To other strugglers, Jason concludes by saying:

I strongly encourage you to pray, like the father in Mark 9:24, "I do believe, help me overcome my unbelief!"

God can change your heart from inside out. God can renew your mind. God can make you a whole new person. Looking back, I am not at all like the person I was in high school in any way, shape or form. I know everybody grows up and changes. But my philosophy, my thoughts, my hunger, my sexuality, everything about me is completely renewed and changed, and I believe I am still being changed into the likeness of the man God wants me to be.

Jesus Christ is truly a God of mercy and grace. Strangely enough, I am now very grateful to have experienced homosexual struggles. When I submitted them to God, I gave him permission to mold and shape me into the man I am today. I am thankful he chose me to help reach out to hurting people, and I'm thankful he granted me the desires of my heart. In him, there are no secrets. He truly is a mighty God. Seek him with all your heart. You will find him. □

6

Living Beyond Denial

Michael Lumberger

*M*ichael Lumberger grew up in the little town of Crabtree, Pennsylvania, a blue-collar, coal-mining town with an overwhelming majority of white faces. The story of his battle with homosexuality, like so many others, begins with feelings of rejection, inadequacy and somehow being "different." It is also another story that reflects how childhood sexual abuse can lead to gender confusion.

Dealing with Racial Prejudice

The youngest child in a family of six children, Mike is ten years younger than his youngest sister. In their hometown of Crabtree there were only four African American families, and two of those families were Mike's relatives. Although he had a number of playmates among the neighborhood children, racial prejudice reared its ugly head early in his life. He recalls playing happily with his friends all day, only to have them angrily called home once their fathers returned from work.

"Those fathers really didn't want their little kids playing with the blacks in our community," Mike explains. "I remember being called names as a kid, but I was still too young to understand racial prejudice and what that all meant."

He goes on to describe an even more difficult challenge:

My problems weren't all outside the home. At four years of age I had an encounter with my older brother. I had awakened from a deep sleep late at night and had wandered downstairs to the kitchen for some water. As I was returning back upstairs to my bedroom, I heard my brother calling me into the room where he was sleeping. He was sitting on the side of his bed in the darkness, undressed and touching his genitals. He asked me to perform a sexual act on him. I was filled with fear and refused. Then he warned me not to say anything to our parents. Little did I know of the sexual confusion that would later follow me into adult life. □

Unfortunately, Mike's fear of his brother's vengeance caused him to avoid going to his mom and dad to somehow explain what had taken place. How could he explain it when he didn't even have the words for what had occurred? "I shut down instead of opening up to my parents for help," he says now with regret.

Mike's father was a hard-working, minority business owner, and his philosophy was best expressed in a proverb: "A man works from sun to sun." He left for work very early in the morning and came back late in the evening. Consequently, Mike didn't have an intimate relationship with his father in which he felt comfortable and at ease. His mother worked too; her job started at ten in the morning, and she returned home at eight each night.

No Sense of Belonging

As the youngest of the children, Mike began to feel "less than" early in life. His racial background, the sexual incident with his brother, and his "afterthought" position in the family caused him to feel as if he didn't belong. And his elementary school experience as part of a mere handful of black children in the school only made matters worse. Race took its toll, and, combined with gender confusion, Mike's self-esteem was always at risk.

As the years passed, I felt increasingly different from other boys. In junior high school I dated girls but sensed a growing fondness for the male body. At the age of thirteen an older friend of mine began to reach out to me. During one of our long phone calls he asked me if I would be interested in having sex with him. I was startled and asked him one question: "Are you queer?" He said, "No, I'm not queer, I just wanted to see where you were."

For the next couple days I kept thinking about that question. Then our next conversation picked up basically right at that same point. I asked a little bit more about where he was in his sexuality. And in that conversation we had made a date to meet one another, and I decided to take him up on his offer. I believe that was my first real homosexual experience.

It was very uncomfortable. I left really confused after that encounter. In my home we didn't have touch, and we didn't hear words of affirmation. That encounter was really different in that it met some needs for touch and affection that had never been met before in my life. □

Mike's gender and identity confusion was also fed by a lack of good family role models. He never saw his dad express any affection for his mother. Similarly, his mom never affirmed his father; instead she criticized and belittled him. Mike's father was a passive man, while his mother was more domineering and controlling.

I don't want to be like him, Mike thought, *and I never want to marry a woman like her.*

Then came 1968. As a high school sophomore Mike began inviting friends to stay overnight at his parents' home as a way of exploring his homosexual curiosity. By the time of his graduation Mike was having weekly encounters with both male and female friends. He had also discovered the world of drugs. Meanwhile, his fantasy world became increasingly perverted. He began looking at other men and women as sex objects, imagining wild orgies that would make him soar sexually, just as the drugs and alcohol made him high and removed from reality.

In college Mike's sexual confusion increased even more. He had three male roommates and two girlfriends, and was sexually involved with all of them at some point. Two of the women and one male roommate declared their love for Mike, but he just laughed it off. For him, whatever was between them was nothing more than sex. Mike was also one of his college's star athletes. "I was afraid of relationships at that time," he recalls, "fearing that they might reveal the darker side of me. So I kept everyone at a distance."

A Terrible Discovery

Mike's homosexual behavior was revealed in a tragic and gruesome incident. After being away on a Thanksgiving holiday, he returned to college to discover that his roommate had slit his wrists. The young man had written a suicide note, lamenting how Mike had rejected his love. Mike's next-door neighbor discovered the bleeding roommate—and the note.

He confronted me. "Lumberger, you had a man!" My heart pounded as he asked, "Are you a faggot?"

Of course, I denied everything, but inside I was already running. Within a week I had packed my bags and left college. I was terrified my athletic friends would find out what I had been doing in secret.

I went back home to work with my family. After months of verbal abuse from family members, which made me feel like a failure, I decided, "If I'm gay, I'm going to be gay all the way." After visiting the gay bars in nearby Pittsburgh, I realized that racism and rejection were also a part of the local gay scene. So I moved to Los Angeles in the hope of ridding myself of memories of the past. □

Wild sexual activity with multiple partners, intense drug use and emotional mood swings marked Mike's time in Los Angeles. When he ran out of money for food and drugs, Mike learned to sell his body on the streets. But after months of fast-paced living he grew sick of the gay scene. Like the New Testament prodigal, he decided, "I'm going home." And he added, "I'm going to find a woman and get married."

And so he did.

In his relationship with his first wife Mike never shared with her any aspect of his sexual struggles. In fact, he had not discussed this aspect of his life with anyone. His church background had taught him that homosexuality was a terrible sin. It had also convinced him that Jesus would wipe away his sins and that once he asked God for forgiveness and returned to the local congregation, he would have no further problems.

Mike naively assumed that God would use the relationship with his wife to strengthen his masculinity. He would then become a man of God, the priest of his home, a godly husband and the future father of children. Mike hid behind the form of Christianity he'd grown up with, unaware of the depth of his problems and confused by the demands of his marriage.

At this point in his life Mike really wanted a relationship with God. And he believed the Bible and all that it said except for one thing—at the core of his being he did not really believe that a homosexual could be free. Meanwhile, he continued to battle with feelings of inadequacy, homosexual urges, and a deep longing to be a good husband and a man of God. He even served as an assistant pastor during this time.

However, three children, several homosexual encounters and four years later Mike decided that maybe he should step aside and spare his family any further wounds. In his mind the marriage was doomed, and he believed that he was ruining the lives of his wife and children. He moved out and plunged headlong once again into the homosexual world. And Mike made a couple of commitments to himself. First, he promised himself that he would never marry again. Second, he vowed that he would never get involved with God again. He began to believe the myth "Once gay, always gay."

A Voice of Authority

After a number of short-lived relationships, Mike met the man of his dreams: an African American who really attracted him. For the first time in his life he truly "fell in love" with someone. Mike made the determination that he would spend the rest of his life with Terry. Together, the two men were happy. And when Mike's children came to visit, they knew Mike's lover as "Uncle" Terry, gravitating to him and learning to cherish him as a family member. For once, Mike was in a monogamous relationship that seemed destined to last. He was happy, he "belonged," and he wanted it to go on forever. He felt complete and wanted everyone—both inside and outside the gay community—to share his happiness.

But then the unexpected happened. The voice of God broke through into Mike's consciousness. It was uninvited. It was, in a sense, unwelcome. And it was authoritative.

One morning I got up after a drunken binge the previous night and heard an inner voice: "It's time to come back home. I need you." Within the week I told my partner, "I really believe that this life and this love affair is coming to a close." I knew that I was in love with Terry; we had been together for three years. But God was drawing my heart to himself. As much as I wanted to resist God, I couldn't.

I started going to church, and eventually Terry gave his heart to the Lord. But our church had some deep problems. It was very legalistic and steeped with secret homosexual activity. Terry and I went our separate ways: I chose to follow God, and Terry chose homosexuality. Then in 1986 I visited Covenant Church of Pittsburgh and sensed God's voice saying, "This is the church where I will deliver you from homosexuality." My reaction was, "Yeah, right!" □

Although Mike felt he heard the voice of hope for his homosexual struggle, he didn't believe God could deliver him. Then a few months later at church his attention was drawn to an attractive woman, and he heard God again: "That woman is going to be your wife."

Mike often watched Benita ministering to others at the front of the church, smiling and raising her hands up in joyful worship and praise. She had an exuberance about her that was very attractive to him. Still, when he thought he heard God say, "She will be your wife," his response was just one word: "Wrong!"

Inevitably, the two were eventually introduced. Mike describes feeling a little leap in his heart when they met. But he also had a strong memory that he was inadequate and an equally strong conviction that he could never marry another woman. Nonetheless, they dated and became fast friends, spending much of their time together. Benita also became great friends with Mike's children. After nine months Mike asked Benita to marry him. She said yes.

Prior to their wedding the two went into premarital counseling, and in Mike's view, the counselor knew that something was going on. He even went so far as to say, "If there is anything in your closet, this is the opportunity for you to open it up and share with the person you plan to spend the rest of your life with." The counselor wanted no skeletons in the closet for either of them to come forth later in their marriage.

But Mike was unmoved. *I'll share everything but this homosexual struggle,* he told himself.

Unfortunately, Mike's former pastor encouraged his silence, saying, "Michael, I would share with her everything except the one struggle with your homosexual past. Most people don't understand the subject. And besides, women tend to use things against you in marriage, especially in times of disagreement. So, I would advise you not to tell her about your homosexual past."

Mike was relieved by this advice, but he kept hearing the Holy Spirit in his heart say, "Share your life with her."

He tenaciously refused to obey.

And so, on a fragile foundation of dishonesty, disobedience and naive enthusiasm Mike began a new marriage with Benita. Soon their first daughter was born. Mike should have been excited and fulfilled. But it wasn't long before his unresolved inner conflicts erupted. He was plagued with gay thoughts, fell into pornography, and on one occasion got together with his former gay lover. Memories from his first marriage began to haunt him. Was it all about to be repeated again?

The Lord challenged Mike again, "The only way you're going to become free of homosexuality is to confess it to your wife. You can't do this on your own."

"Lord, I'm not going there," Mike protested.

Several months later the Lord challenged Mike again, and again he refused. Finally, Mike sensed an ultimatum: "You are either going to tell your wife of your homosexual sin, or I'm going to start taking away those things that you love the most."

By now Mike owned a trucking business that was making a tidy profit. His trucks alone ranged in price from fifty to a hundred thousand dollars each—and he had ten of them. Mike's company was in demand all over the city of Pittsburgh. Then, without any warning, clutches and transmissions and other problems began disabling the vehicles. At the same time, customer cancellations and distraught workers came out of nowhere. Within a few months Mike's corporation was staring at possible bankruptcy.

In the meantime the rest of his world continued to come crashing down. Finances soon became the least of his worries. He tried to purchase a life insurance policy. The blood test caused him to be rejected. He tried another company. And another. At the bottom of the rejection notice was an asterisk and a note: "Please see a physician for further information." Upon inquiry his doctor said soberly: "Michael, the reason you're being rejected for life insurance is because you test positive for the AIDS virus."

Mike went in for testing, then waited weeks for the results. The wait was agonizing. Finally he went back for the results and received the news he feared most: his test was positive for AIDS antibodies. His doctor offered words of assurance that good medical treatment was available and that AIDS was not an automatic death sentence. After he left the doctor's office, Mike sat in his car and cried uncontrollably for two hours, unable to drive. He kept hearing a still, small voice saying, "But, Michael, all of this is for a reason. I have need of you in the kingdom."

Mike answered, "God, what the heck are you talking about? I'm so frustrated. I don't know who I am as a man. I don't even know why I got married again."

Yet the thought wouldn't leave him. "Michael, I have need of you in the kingdom. If you'll tell your wife of your sexual struggle, I'll set you free."

Mike retorted, "God, this is unfair. I *can't* tell her!"

The voice of God persisted, "If you confess to your wife, I'll set you free."

Mike went home but couldn't bring himself to offer Benita a simple, straightforward confession. He was silent for months, even entering into unsafe sex with her. Certainly if he started using condoms, she would ask why, and Mike would have to confess his past. The inner turmoil was excruciating.

I felt as though I had become schizoid. I could no longer think of what was right to do. I was losing everything—or so it seemed. Finally, on Memorial Day of 1988, I felt the Lord say to me, "Today is your day to begin confessing. The truth shall set you free." I was fearful of the consequences—but I obeyed this time. □

"Honey," Mike began, "I want to tell you some of the things I practiced before you and I were married." He mentioned homosexuality in a long list of other things.

"Don't worry about it, Mike," she told him. "We all have skeletons in our closets." She didn't seem upset at all.

But the next day, it hit her: *My husband was involved in homosexual-*

ity! Benita went directly to the family pastor. He sent her home with one piece of advice: "Ask Michael to tell you the whole story." Later, fear gripped Mike's heart as Benita shared what the pastor had directed her to ask him.

Coming to Terms with Denial

Mike told his wife a little bit more but couldn't bring himself to tell everything. A few days later the pastor asked them to come in for an appointment. He wanted a full confession, and Mike knew once and for all that he had to come clean with the truth.

As he spilled the entire, sordid story of his past, he saw anger rising in his wife, an anger that he'd never seen in anyone before. Eventually she controlled herself and forgave Mike, but, to say the least, the session wasn't easy for either of them. Mike felt totally emasculated. He couldn't imagine going to men's meetings at the church because now that his secret was out, he didn't feel like a real man. He was plagued with gay memories. It seemed like all the demons of hell had been unleashed against him that day. At the pastor's request Mike participated in a support group. He was willing to do whatever it took to restore his shaken marriage.

At first he hated attending Living Waters, a support group for ex-gays right in his own church. The leader of the group was very effeminate, and Mike found it extremely distracting. He also had to come to grips with the fact that everyone was attending the group for one main reason: to find freedom from homosexual addiction. But then something happened.

One night the teaching really got through to me. I began to understand the underlying reasons for my addiction. Over the next year I kept attending the group, and my life improved greatly. It was in that group that I first found hope. They helped me deal with issues of my past that I'd never dealt with before—especially the roots of my homosexuality.

I came to see that my dad and mom had done the best that they could with the little bit that they'd had. The ongoing lessons I learned from Living

Waters helped me face my environment, my peers, and who I was as a person.

But there was something else I learned in the group that, I guess, I didn't allow myself to learn early on—and that was seeking the face of God. If I was ever going to walk away from homosexuality or the homosexual struggle, I would need the power of the cross. God said, "Whoever my son sets free is free indeed," and I needed to believe that his Son had the ability to set me free—and the ability to keep me free.

The challenge lay in my unwillingness to obey his word. I knew that I needed to practice the presence of the Almighty, and I made it a point to wake up every day and seek God's face before my family got up. I sought him in his word and in prayer. And I did that consistently. God was revealing to me his purpose for my sexuality, and I was taking it seriously. I started believing there was hope for me. □

Then Mike received a call from the sister of a former lover. She asked Mike to visit her brother, who had become very ill.

Keith was dying of AIDS in the hospital. We began talking, and our conversation went deep. "Where did it all go wrong?" I asked him.

"It went wrong when I didn't accept Jesus." He had never mentioned Jesus in all the years I'd known him.

"If you had it all to do over again, what would you do differently?"

He looked at me sadly and said, "I would not be a homosexual. This has been a painful life for me."

I held his pitiful body in my arms and tears slid down my face as I asked him to forgive me for all the unholy things we had done together. As we talked, he fell silent and limp. I realized that he had died right in my arms.

Later as I stumbled out to my car, I wondered, "God, why did you do that to me?" When I started my car engine, the radio came on and I heard a well-known Bible teacher say, "You were chosen for such a time as this. And you will lead many to redemption." □

A Matter of Life and Death

Meanwhile, by 1995 Mike's battle for his health began to intensify.

When he went to his doctor's office for his annual checkup, the doctor said, "Mike, have you considered going on AZT?"

"No." Mike shook his head. "I don't need that yet."

A month later the doctor took another test, and once the results came back, he asked the question, "Your T-cells have dropped a little bit more. Would you consider AZT?"

Finally, in June 1995, Mike asked, "Doctor, you keep asking me month after month whether I would consider AZT. Why?"

"Well, Mike, it's because your T-cells have dropped to ten." Mike was stunned when the doctor went on to say, "You have full-blown AIDS."

The next weekend Mike accompanied the church's youth group to a camp in Washington, D.C. He was feeling weak and couldn't keep up with the group's schedule. The following week he attended his brother-in-law's funeral in New York. At a friend's home he asked if he could lie down. He passed out for hours. When the friend inquired about his health, Mike simply said, "I'm exhausted." Still unable to cope with the truth he never thought to attribute his exhaustion to the doctor's alarming diagnosis.

Mike knew that he wasn't physically strong. Over the past six months his weight had been steadily dropping. So, once he returned home, Mike realized that he would have to tell Benita the news about his condition. She already knew that there was a good possibility that Mike would someday contract full-blown AIDS. Now Mike informed her that the time had come. He saw the look of panic on her face and did what he could to comfort her. Together they told Bishop Garlington, their senior pastor, and his wife about Mike's circumstances.

Mike was in and out of the hospital over the next year. He was in the hospital for Thanksgiving, home for Christmas Day, then back in hospital the day after Christmas, where he spent the whole of New Year's Day. After that hospitalization he found himself lying on his bed, very weak, not knowing if he was going to live or die. He remembers:

One afternoon my six-year-old daughter, Amy, walked into my bedroom after school and looked at me. I had a book lying next to me called Roger's Story, *which is about AIDS.*

She looked at me, then she looked at the book, contemplating whether or not to ask the question that was upon her mind. Finally she said, "Daddy, do you have AIDS?"

I knew that I shouldn't lie to her, yet I was fearful of what would happen if I shared the truth.

I answered, "Yes, I have AIDS."

Amy instantly passed out. I was so weak that I couldn't move to help her, and I didn't know what to do. Finally she got up and she said, "Daddy, are you going to die?"

I said, "No, Amy. I don't believe I'm going to die. God has already made a promise to me from Psalm 118: 'You will live and not die, and declare the works of the Lord.' I honestly believe that God is going to give me enough strength to walk you down the aisle one day when you are a bride."

"Are you sure God said you're going to live?" she asked.

"All I can hold on to is the word that God gave me, that's all I have, Amy."
She gave me a hug and walked out of the room. □

Despite the reason behind Mike's sickness, Benita never brought up to him his homosexual past. She never made him feel that he deserved all that was happening to him. Through all of it she maintained a spirit of grace and mercy. Today Mike continues to affirm that he has never witnessed such kindness in all his life.

One day Benita and Mike agreed that they needed to tell the church about the illness. Mike was going back into the hospital that same day. "I can't do it now," Mike explained. "I don't have the strength to stand before the congregation and share our struggle. If sharing is what we have to do, you've got to do it for us."

In Mike's stead Benita stood before the congregation of two thousand people. She described the struggle they had been through, and she told what it was like to be married to a former homosexual and later to have to live with the secrecy of his illness.

She had no idea how the congregation would respond. Afterward the church rose up, embraced her and rallied around the Lumbergers. "Covenant Church became our family," Benita said later.

Words of Hope and Promise

Mike was still trying to continue his homeopathic treatment. He went to Raleigh to see a doctor, intending to try bio-oxidative medicine and spent forty-five days in treatment. For the first time he thought there might be a glimmer of hope. But in July 1996 the doctor shook his head and said, "Michael, we've done everything possible to keep you from going on the meds, but there is this cocktail drug out that I believe will work for you. We've got to try something else. You are in the final stages of this disease. Your next step is death—unless we try something new."

We started the cocktail drug in July. It wasn't terribly effective. It was keeping me alive and my T-cell count went from zero up to five, but it never went higher. I was still very weak through the rest of that year.

Then in October 1996 an evangelist named Mary Ann Brown gave me a prophetic word that Satan had done everything in his power to destroy my life through sickness and disease. She said this without knowing a thing about me. Then she recalled the same Scripture that God had given me that I would live and not die, and declare the works of the Lord. I remember the cheers of the congregation—it was like being in a football stadium when your home team scores the winning touchdown. The roar was amazing!

Immediately after that word I was hospitalized again. I prayed, "God, is your word real? Are you going to do what you said?"

I was tired of fighting. But I felt within my spirit that the Lord said, "You are going to live and not die." □

Somewhere between October and December of 1996 Mike's T-cells went up a bit. They reached a point between 10 and 15. Then during the first half of the next year they shot up to 68. At the same time, his viral load, which had been in the millions, plummeted to zero.

To Mike's amazement his doctor reported, "Michael, according to your viral load, you are now nondetectable."

"What does that mean?" Mike asked.

"It means that although the virus still resides within you, its levels are so low that we can't find it anymore."

At last Mike was able to say with full assurance, "I *am* going to live! I'm *not* going to die!" Soon afterward he told his church about the victory of Jesus Christ in his life and all that God had done.

The next two years were a time of reconciliation and healing for the Lumberger family. Mike went to work mending relationships, especially with his three oldest children, who were all out of the house by then. Christmas 1998 was the first holiday during which all his children from both marriages came together as one large family. Up until then far too many Christmas Days had been centered on whether or not Mike was going to live. But that year Benita and Mike were instead able to buy gifts for everyone, celebrating both the birth of Christ and the gift of new life Mike had received.

Today Mike is director of Dunamis Ministries, an ex-gay outreach, and a member of the pastoral staff at Covenant Church of Pittsburgh. The changes God has brought about in his life are amazing and miraculous, he says:

Because of God's abundant grace and his miraculous power to heal, I walk totally free from the AIDS virus. My wife and I will celebrate fourteen years of marriage this year.

Without the Lord, my life would have never changed.

With him, I have learned that all things are possible. □

7

Words of Wisdom,
Words of Love

Patty Wells Graham

*P*atty Graham's involvement in lesbianism and her departure
from it are unique in several ways. Patty's experience with homosexuality did not originate with the typical family dynamics that
exist in many other people's lives. She had a stable relationship with
both her parents, and she was never molested.

Patty was the oldest child and the only girl in her family, which
gave her a special place—at least until the birth of her younger
brother. After that Patty didn't feel quite as important, and at times
it seemed to her that her mother actually liked boys better than
girls. Still, the family was close and loving, and they attended
church together. Patty explains:

*My relationship with my mom was not strikingly negative or positive.
There was not a real strong connection between us, and there was a lot of com-*

*petition. I think that competition was what ultimately drove me apart from
her. I was always trying to be as good and fun and cute as she was, and I could
never quite make it. That was a strong factor in our relationship.*

*Another part of the equation was that my parents have always been
extremely close. There are some very wonderful things about that, which I am
now emulating. But there were some very negative things as well because it
tended to be a symbiotic closeness so that nobody else could really get in there
and relate to either Mom or Dad separately. You had to relate to the "unit" of
Mom and Dad. Consequently, there was no opportunity for me to connect with
Mom like I really needed to. I think that pushed me in the direction of becoming emotionally dependent on other women. I was trying to find that connection with "woman-ness" that I didn't have with my own mom.* □

Steps into Feminism

From Patty's perspective, another negative aspect of her family's
behavior was the practice of open nudity in the home. Today she
remembers that nudity as something she never felt quite right
about, something she didn't like but was unable to change. The
problems it caused didn't surface until she was older. But the sexual
stimulation that occurred because of other family members being
openly nude at home left her feeling guilty for years and contributed to chronic depression and low self-esteem.

At age eleven, at a Youth For Christ rally, Patty Wells accepted
Jesus Christ as her Savior. She immediately experienced loving
Jesus and being fully loved by him, but she never fully grasped the
idea of obedience or learning to overcome personal sin. "Looking
back," she says, "I realize I never understood the power that the
Holy Spirit gives us to deal with the sin in our lives." She continues:

*My family experience with nudity eventually led me to equate being special
and being close to people with being sexual. In junior high and high school I
was plagued with masturbation. It seemed to control me. I was sexually pro-
miscuous in college. This was all going on while I was trying to walk with
God.* □

Patty knew that marrying an unbeliever wasn't scriptural, but she dated boys who weren't Christians anyway. And she inevitably became serious about one of the young men she dated. She married him in 1969.

Because of her battle with low self-esteem, she recalls, she expected her new husband to make her feel both important and valued, a need that she now realizes only God could meet. But without a proper foundation and spiritual unity, the marriage eventually deteriorated. Patty sought psychological counseling because of her marital problems. By the time she decided to seek help, she had already given up on her marriage and decided to divorce her husband. She focused her therapeutic attention on seeking a satisfying life for herself.

During the early 1970s feminism was on the rise as a cultural movement. And it quickly got Patty's attention.

Feminism appealed to me very much at this point because it promised personal power to women. It provided emotional support at a time when I was convinced that only other women could understand me. With my damaged self-esteem, that counterfeit power and emotional strength was inviting. The step into lesbianism from there was easy as my determination to identify with women grew. I eventually became sexually involved with my best friend of ten years. We were fighting together for our rights as women. Since she had been the person in my life most able to understand my intimate thoughts and feelings, she seemed the ideal partner for me.

But even my best friend and fellow struggler, though she adored me, did not satisfy my need to be special. I wanted more, though I didn't know what that meant. I went looking for it by indulging simultaneously in another lesbian relationship. The self-indulgence seemed fulfilling, but it wasn't enough. I still wasn't satisfied. □

Coming Out with the Truth

Patty's coming out to her parents as a lesbian happened unexpectedly. Rather than being her idea, the revelation was initiated by her

dad. Her parents had seen a program on *Phil Donahue* featuring lesbians and discussing their relationships. Until then, although they'd
been aware of gay men, Patty's mom and dad had never known that
lesbians existed. But during a visit home Patty's father took her
aside—her communication with him was more open than with her
mother—and he told her that they had seen the show. "Lesbians—
that's what the show was about. And that's what you and Karen are,
isn't it?" he asked.

Patty was speechless. What should she say? What *could* she say?

At first the freedom to be real with her father was wonderful,
and because her mother wasn't present, she was able to be unusu-
ally open and honest with him. He asked questions, and she
unashamedly answered them as honestly as possible. His questions
reflected to her what seemed to be genuine interest and concern.
"How did this happen?" he wondered. "How does your relationship
work?" "What really goes on?" Her father couldn't have been more
loving and accepting. And, in response, Patty made herself vulnerable to him.

Then he suggested that they include Patty's mother (who had
been taking a nap) in the conversation. One of the first things she
said when Patty told her what they'd been talking about was, "Oh,
I've always known that about you."

The words cut through Patty like a knife. Despite her apparent
comfort in her relationship with Karen, her mother's words rang
with disdain, resounding a lifelong rejection of who Patty was. "It
wasn't just my behavior I heard her scorning, but it was who I am
in the world. Her response to me and my response to her words
became a real wedge between us."

That was the end of the discussion. And from that time on,
Patty's parents—who never liked talking about unpleasant things
anyway—simply pretended that Patty's situation didn't exist. They
also acted as if Karen, Patty's partner, didn't exist. They refused to
talk to Karen when they phoned Patty. And they refused to talk
about her in subsequent conversations. "It was like she was a

ghost," Patty recalls.

When Patty's parents sent letters to their daughter, they mailed them to her workplace. They did everything they could to obliterate Patty's personal life from their consciousness. And although she could more or less understand their anger and repulsion, the communication between them during Patty's ten years of lesbianism was sparse.

However, this strained relationship provided some interesting insights into Patty's own inner life. She explains:

I had moved out to San Francisco from North Carolina, three thousand miles away from my parents, to pursue my chosen lifestyle. For the first couple of years I had intense, almost obsessive thoughts about how unreasonable it was that they were responding the way they were and how they were rejecting me. I felt a deep resentment and anger, almost a hatred, for them. These intense feelings and obsessive thoughts went on all the time. They clouded everything I did.

I am a psychotherapist by profession, and it finally occurred to me that these feelings were a little more intense than the situation warranted. The idea dawned on me that I was projecting onto them my own conflict about being involved in homosexuality. As I got that, my conflict and resentment toward my parents vanished. □

Not long after that dramatic turning point Karen and Patty decided to split up, and Patty leased her own apartment, which proved to be a further step into self-indulgence. Living alone she could do exactly what she wanted to do whenever she wanted to do it. Once she had her own residence, "my time was my own and so was my space."

Words of Wisdom
In her search for herself, Patty looked for answers beyond the political (feminism) and physical (sexual expression) realms. She dabbled in things that were "spiritual" but that denied the deity of

Jesus Christ. During high school and college she had retained a relationship with the Lord. During her marriage she had tried to follow Christ, but it was not easy because her husband didn't share her religious life. Ironically, in order to walk out of her marriage Patty had left the Lord behind. She continued to deny him until November of 1984, when she was diagnosed with a breast tumor. She recalls:

I couldn't believe it. At that very time a close friend of mine was dying of breast cancer. Worse yet, I had just learned that my mom had metastasized breast cancer. I was terrified.

During my month of waiting for surgery my Christian brother told me that he had received a word of wisdom from God for me—that I should go to Calvary Chapel in San Francisco for healing prayer. He told me what to say and what to do. I was willing to try anything because I was scared, really scared.

Although I had been away from church for many years, I went to Calvary Chapel in San Francisco and the elders there prayed for me. I experienced a renewed hunger for God. The tumor did not go away, but it was not malignant, as the doctors had feared it might be. I'm thankful for that, but the major healing had occurred elsewhere—in my heart. I knew I had come home to the Lord. Now I needed to figure out how to fit all the parts of my life together.

As a gay person I felt strange in a church of heterosexual believers. I tried a gay church for a while but sensed the Spirit of God was hindered there, and I wanted the Spirit in his fullness. So I returned to Calvary Chapel.

In April I asked the Lord if I was still saved after being away from him for so long. Deep in my heart I heard a resounding yes. A week later I asked Jesus to be Lord of my life. I dove into church activities to get all the teaching and fellowship I could, telling people all along the way of my gayness, testing the waters. Lo and behold, they still loved and accepted me! There was no judgmentalism. □

On June 3, 1985, Patty went out to dinner with a man in her church's home fellowship. He told her that she needed to be healed of her homosexuality. At first that sounded very strange to Patty. She thought, *If God wants that, I'll certainly do it. But I haven't heard anything from him about it!*

But the next morning she woke up with a strong conviction that she needed deliverance. She called her Christian brother and asked him to pray with her. As he prayed, she trembled all over. She didn't understand what was happening; she simply knew that it was important.

All day she felt empty, as though she'd lost her best friend. (She later realized that a part of her had indeed died with that prayer.) About 3:00 in the afternoon, sitting alone in her office for the first time that day, she prayed, "Lord, why do I feel so bad? Didn't I do something good?" Immediately the Holy Spirit brought to mind part of a verse she hadn't heard or read for more than a decade: "Old things are passed away; behold, all things are become new" (2 Corinthians 5:17). All at once the emptiness left, and she felt filled up and complete once again. From that point on Patty Wells knew she was on the right track. The change in her life was a process, one that didn't happen overnight. But from that day on she was decidedly motivated to walk away from homosexuality. To obey God in this way—in every way—became her delight.

When asked how her experience might help others who struggle to leave homosexual behavior behind, she says:

First and foremost, it is so essential to draw close to the Lord. That has been absolutely, without a doubt, the most central feature of my healing process. I had to let him redefine my identity and speak the feminine into my life. So that's been the most critical. For the last couple of years I've been practicing "listening prayer." And that has been so important, just to be quiet before the Lord so that he can speak into my life.

The second thing I had to learn was to stand on my own and not be emotionally dependent in relationships. The first seven years after I came back to the Lord, I was not in an intimate relationship. In fact, until I met my husband, I had no romantic relationships. And I'm so grateful for that, for it allowed me to walk away from that tendency to rely on relationships with others to be my "be all and end all."

If you'd asked me when I was in lesbianism what was the most important thing, I would have said "intimacy." But it really wasn't intimacy I was seeking at that time. It was emotional dependence, which had become a god for me. Now that I'd left that behind, standing on my own was really important.

It was also key for me to have close and caring relationships with a variety of godly women—not just with one woman and not a sexual relationship. That's how I have learned what God intends for relationships with the same sex.

Perhaps most indispensable to my new life was healing for my wounded relationship with my mom, or what is sometimes called "mother wounding." There have been many steps along the way.

One day I was having some healing prayer and was asked to "speak forgiveness" to my mother. I couldn't do it! The words wouldn't come out. Suddenly all I could feel was anger and unforgiveness, which provided me with a way of feeling powerful with her. Finally I was able to express some of that through the healing prayer, just through crying and letting go of the anger. Along the way there has also been some grieving over the loss of the "ideal mother."

My mother was always so "potent" a figure for me—so powerful, in fact, that I felt like I was always in her shadow. Even until recently my image of my mom was that she was great big, and I was kind of little and lost. □

The Love of a Lifetime

Patty has since been much more able to separate from her mother and truly forgive her. She has also learned to deal with sins of self-hatred, envy (hence all the competition between the two females) and misogyny (the hatred of women). Patty gained a clear sense that these had been passed down to her through her mom, and to her mother from Patty's grandmother, and so on for several generations.

At the same time Patty came to recognize in her mother a zest and enthusiasm for life, which she had also inherited, and she treasures that love of life as a gift. She also learned from her mother the ability to be devoted to her husband—an attribute that has greatly benefited Patty's new marriage.

She points out with a smile that being married has provided a wonderful means of healing for her.

I have a husband who really embraces me and adores me, and it's been the crowning touch on my healing process. Since the beginning of our relationship he has often exclaimed, "You are such a woman!" That has been so wonderful for me to take in and receive as part of my healing.

Since leaving lesbianism behind, my life has not been the same. The most incredible gift the Lord is giving me is the knowledge that I am special to him—really special in the way I've always longed to be. He is with me all the time ("I will never leave you nor forsake you," Joshua 1:5), and he gives me his whole attention ("Let him have all your worries and cares, for he is always thinking about you and watching over everything that concerns you," 1 Peter 5:7 LB). The Bible says that God has numbered the hairs on my head. He is concerned about the smallest details of my life. My need for attention is finally, fully satisfied in this most intimate of relationships.

Knowing his very special love has become a theme in my walk with God, as has learning obedience. From the day of my prayer for deliverance from homosexuality, I have been learning that God requires obedience, and he greatly rewards it.

"If you obey my commands, you will remain in my love, just as I have obeyed my Father's commands and remain in his love. I have told you this so that my joy may be in you and that your joy may be complete" (John 15:10-11).

It's true—my joy is complete! Learning obedience has been an adventure. Yielding to him has become a joy and satisfaction I never thought possible. ☐

8

Hope for a
Struggling Marriage

Tye & Nancy Gamey

T ye and Nancy Gamey are one couple whose marriage has survived a multitude of storms very similar to those that have devastated thousands of other marriages. Even though Tye was sexually unfaithful after their wedding day, God has preserved their relationship. Today that relationship is a solid foundation for their ministry together as leaders of an ex-gay ministry in Winnipeg, Canada.

Here is how Tye describes his early childhood struggles, which eventually led him into same-sex encounters and years of turmoil and despair:

Much of my childhood memory involves spending a lot of time helping my mother and being in the feminine world. I felt very safe and comfortable there. And so I think because of that I picked up some very effeminate mannerisms.

These were the typical stereotypes of a prehomosexual child: the limp wrist, the high voice with sort of a squeak in it and a wiggle in my walk.

I don't think I was aware of these outward effeminate mannerisms when I was a young child, but there was a sense of feeling quite different. For one thing, my family was expecting a girl when I was born. Growing up I felt very comfortable playing with the girls or helping my mom in the kitchen or being with my aunts when there were family gatherings.

So, when it came to spending time with the boys, there was always a sense of Am I going to fit in? Do I really belong here? □

When Tye talks about his struggle with homosexuality, he has much to tell us. He struggled with his same-sex peer relationships. He was also the victim of repeated sexual abuse. But today when he shares his story, he doesn't just discuss the problems he faced in childhood. He talks about his marriage—the valiant battle his wife, Nancy, and he have faced to keep their marriage together.

Because the battle with homosexuality so often involves the entire family, in this chapter both Tye and Nancy will share their insights about their marriage and the difficulties they have faced over many years. But first it's important for us to understand a little more about Tye's early life and the events that helped to shape his gender confusion.

The mannerisms Tye describes caused him to face mocking and belittlement during puberty, and this became a constant source of embarrassment to him, particularly after he became a freshman in high school. Meanwhile, his desire for male companionship led him into the company of boys who were sexually adventurous. A game of strip poker, which resulted first in the taking off of clothing and later in same-sex physical contact, both excited and shamed Tye.

But the worst was yet to come. Tye recalls:

During that time there was an older gentleman in our community who, I later found out, was referred to as the "town homosexual." One day he offered to give me a ride in his car. "Sure," I said, and I walked around to the passen-

ger side and climbed in. We were driving down a country road, and he was fairly friendly, talking and laughing. Then, all of a sudden, he reached over and began rubbing my leg and groin area. All this quickly led to sexual pleasure, and this was my first sexual experience with an older person. But I felt bad about it afterward, blaming myself and realizing that it shouldn't have happened.

Some time later, my brothers and dad were talking about stuff going on in the community and this man's name came up. They started saying that he was a homosexual.

And then my dad said, "Whatever you do, stay away from him."

By then it was a little late. And I wasn't about to tell anyone what had happened. □

Despite his sexual experimentation and that first molestation, Tye was still interested in dating girls. But when he asked a classmate whether she would be willing to go out with him, he found himself both rejected and humiliated. She made a point of letting him know that he was the last person on earth she would ever want to go out with.

This was followed by a couple of encounters with another older homosexual that, because of the pleasurable sensations involved, led to a sequence of anonymous sexual encounters. All this happened before Tye had reached the twelfth grade.

But another important encounter took place at the same time. This encounter was the one that would change Tye's life once and for all.

In my final year of high school I had a friend who came from a Christian home, and she invited me to some youth meetings. There was a presentation of the gospel and an altar call. I went forward for prayer and made a commitment to Jesus Christ. It was really a high experience, and I threw away my cigarettes and vowed that I wasn't going to do this or do that ever again.

That lasted about two or three weeks, and then I was smoking again and just sort of continuing on my life the way it had been.

But not long afterward the same friend was going off to a Christian conference at a Bible college. I went along. As before, there was a speaker who gave a gospel message and an altar call. I'm glad they sang one more verse of "Just as I Am," because I walked across about ten or twelve people's legs to get out to the aisle and go up to the front.

I explained to the pastor that I had done this before, but it just hadn't lasted. This time I was talked through the process carefully and prayerfully. After that there was a real significant change in my life, and Jesus became very, very vibrant.

But at the same time, my involvement with homosexuality and my ambivalence about it seemed to increase. Sometimes this meant that I would head for the city, cruising and getting involved in homosexual activity. Sometimes it meant that I was simply consumed with thoughts of homosexual fantasy, lust and masturbation. On the other hand, I had made a commitment to Christ, and I was trying to be nice, to be a good Christian boy.

This was my last year of high school, grade twelve, and I had just turned eighteen. ☐

Following these difficult and ambiguous circumstances, Tye enrolled in Bible school, where his personal confusion became even more pronounced. On the one hand, he was taking Bible classes and involving himself in a very energetic Christian community. On the other, he was involved in anonymous homosexual activities when he was away from the campus. But all the while, like so many others who struggle with sin while deeply yearning for God, little by little Tye was growing in his faith. His understanding of God's Word was deepening. His desire to know and serve God was becoming very important to him.

Then came an opportunity to participate in a drama group, which meant taking the gospel message to Asia and the Indian subcontinent. This was a dream come true for Tye, who had always been attracted to drama. And although he still faced homosexual fantasies during the year-long ministry trip, he began to sense a weakening of his physical cravings. He even considered a career of ongoing missionary work in India.

However, when he returned home, Tye got reinvolved in homosexual behavior. As Tye's faith increased, he began to promise God, "Honestly. This time is the last time." How desperately he wanted to change! Every sexual encounter was followed by regret and emotional repentance. The pattern was excruciating. He didn't know where to turn for help, so Tye tried to stop what he was doing cold turkey. He wasn't successful.

In his exhausting struggle between homosexuality and faith, Tye had a longing to marry and begin a family. He wondered if he would be able to respond to a woman's interest, so focused had he been on male attention. He hoped against hope that he would be. He wrestled mightily with himself.

"God, when I meet the girl that you have for me," I prayed, "open my eyes and hit me on the head with a bowling ball. Or strike me with a lightning bolt. Just make sure that I see her when she comes so that I don't miss her, because I do believe that you have somebody for me."

I first noticed Nancy when she walked into a church college and career meeting. I told myself, "Now here's someone I would like to get to know."

So, we started to get acquainted. One time a group of the college and career people went out for lunch, and they had planned afterward to go to a movie. I didn't really want to do what they were going to do, and Nancy didn't either.

I suggested to Nancy, "Do you want to come over to my place for tea?" And she said, "Sure."

And as we were going to my place, inside my head I'm thinking, Oh, God, I hope she doesn't think I'm interested. I'm just a friend.

Later on I found out that she was thinking exactly the same thing. □

After one of the couple's first meetings Tye went home, lay down on his bed and stared at the ceiling. He couldn't help but wonder if this woman Nancy was the answer to his prayers. He had asked God to make sure that he would recognize the right one when she came along, the woman who would be his wife. Tye had pleaded with God to make sure he didn't miss her. Was this it?

Tye had long ago promised the Lord that he would share his struggle with the woman God sent to him. He didn't want to hide it from her. So when he found himself sitting on the front steps of the house where Nancy was living, sharing aspects of their lives with one another, Tye allowed the conversation to turn toward his battle with homosexuality. He told Nancy a great deal about it. But he did so as if it were all in the past. Perhaps that's what he really wanted to believe—that it was over and behind him. Or perhaps that's all his deep denial would allow him to say.

Nancy recalls that conversation:

When Tye told me about his struggle, I was surprised but not especially shocked. I was honored that he would confide in me. When I was a teenager, I'd had a friend who was a lesbian. I had gotten along well with her, so I wasn't horrified by the idea that Tye struggled with homosexuality. But I did feel that it was something that was not natural. I didn't think that God had created Tye to be gay. And if God didn't like it, then he would also provide a way out of it.

I also believed that if some of his sexual needs were met within marriage, then he wouldn't have to go out and have other encounters with guys. I thought, If this is really God's plan for us, then we will get through it. I also thought that it was possible that deep down he was just being rebellious toward God. Once he got through that, I reasoned, he'd be just fine.

Later I came to see that this is one of the things that naive people think because they don't really understand the struggle. It wasn't until much later—five years later—that I actually began to understand that he was really attracted to men in the same way that I was attracted to men.

Meanwhile, as we spent more time together, I began to fall in love. But Tye was talking about going to India on a mission assignment, and it was obvious that I was not a part of his plans. By this time we had become very close, so I decided to be blunt: "I would love to go to India with you, but not as a single person." □

The revelation that Nancy wanted to marry Tye came to him as a total shock. Superficially he was thrilled; marriage was something he had always wanted. But although he had confided in Nancy about his past struggles with homosexuality, what Nancy didn't know was that he was still having occasional gay encounters.

Each time, of course, Tye promised himself that it would be his last. And in a sense he was as naïve as Nancy. Somehow he thought marriage would be the quick cure for all his sexual struggles. But just before their wedding on December 28, 1981, fears momentarily flooded over him. *Dear God, I hope I can do this!* he thought. But he put the idea out of his mind and went ahead anyway.

Nancy had her own fears. As she walked down the aisle, her knees were shaking. She thought, *I hope I'm making the right decision. It's too late to turn back.* Like Tye, she set her doubts aside and made her way down the aisle.

Three months after the wedding Tye had sex with another man. And he knew that he had to tell Nancy. Naturally, she was devastated. She reflects on that conversation:

I felt like my insides were being ripped to shreds. All my life I had been taught that I shouldn't have problems if I was living a victorious Christian life. If things went wrong, I thought there was something wrong with me. So in this case, I somehow concluded that I wasn't a good enough wife to keep Tye sexually faithful. The pain was so overwhelming that I went into denial, telling myself that if I just tried harder and trusted God more, everything would be okay.

As a result, I totally turned inward. I couldn't tell anybody about this part of our lives together. Meanwhile, I was devastated by his unfaithfulness, just three months after we were married. I wanted to leave. I wanted to get out. I wanted to run away, but I had nowhere to go. I had no one to turn to because nobody knew about Tye's problem

In my despair I told him that I didn't want him to ever tell me anything like this again because I just couldn't handle it. And so for the next five years we just stuffed everything. We put everything on the shelf. I told myself that things were getting better. I also continued to tell myself if I just prayed harder and trusted God a little more that everything would be okay.

In the meantime Tye was still struggling and having sexual falls. We went overseas as missionaries to India for a period of almost three years. He even had sexual falls when he was there, although at the time I was unaware of them. And a large part of that unawareness was because I just didn't want to know. ☐

Fortunately, once the Gameys returned to Canada, they sought Christian counseling to help them sort out their marital problems. This happened while they were making preparations to go overseas for a more permanent mission assignment. During the first session the counselor centered most of his attention on Nancy. During the second session he did the same. Nancy recalls:

Once the third session rolled around, he was still spending a lot of time on me, and I was getting angry because I thought, We came here for Tye's problem, not mine. What does this have to do with me?

But as things unfolded, I began to see that I had some issues that needed to be dealt with. First and foremost was our communication. We could talk about a lot of things, but they were all superficial. We couldn't talk about things in our hearts that really mattered to us—particularly Tye's sexual struggle.

So Tye and I started going out weekly for coffee. We'd just talk about the week and how things had gone. We started working on issues like encouraging each other and trying to understand each other. At the same time, we also went through a course on marriage counseling and discovered where we had misread each other, how we had projected our own likes and dislikes onto one another. ☐

During the counseling process Tye and Nancy also learned that a major root cause of Tye's uncontrollable sexual behavior was his childhood sexual abuse. He had never learned how to fill his relational emptiness with men except through sex. Somehow he had to learn how to get past a number of barriers between himself and closeness with other men. He had to see that his same-sex emotional needs were met in healthy ways.

While the counseling process continued, Tye's sexual falls became less frequent. As time went on, he came to believe that six months of sexual faithfulness was quite an accomplishment for him. Perhaps it was the best he could hope for. And he and Nancy became more honest about his seemingly endless struggles.

In 1990 the Gameys heard about Exodus International and decided to attend their first Exodus conference. Both of them dreamed that this conference would be a turning point in their painful marriage. Amazingly, in the midst of all their troubles they had even begun to hope that they could have their own ministry to those who struggled with homosexuality. Nancy remembers the conference very clearly:

It was at the conference, about the third or fourth day, that Tye shared with me that he'd fallen into another sexual encounter. It had happened the week before the conference. I had already gone ahead of him with our youngest child, who was still a small baby. Tye had been left behind in Winnipeg on his own when it happened.

This is when I actually came to the end of myself. I thought, We have worked for four years on our issues. I thought we were farther along than this. I thought we were ready to launch a ministry. I thought God had asked me to stay in this marriage. I thought we were going to minister together.

And all of a sudden, I didn't trust myself anymore. I thought, Maybe I didn't really hear from God after all. Maybe I was just hearing what I wanted to hear.

During that conference I told God, "I don't know what you want from me anymore. I don't know if you want me to stay in the marriage. I don't feel like I have anything left to give. If you want me to leave, I don't know how I'm going to make it because I have three children, and one of them is an infant. I can't go out and work because I've got these dependents. But I know if you want me to leave, I'll be OK because I know you are with me."

I also said, "If you want me to stay with him, I'll stay, because if you're with me, that's where I want to be."

When I went to a women's support group, which was essentially for wives, one of the ladies told me, "You need to be willing to leave him." I was so angry with her! I thought, How could you tell me that? You don't know what my situation is. *And yet I really believe that she was being completely truthful. I had to be willing to leave him, and by then I was.*

The woman concluded by saying, "But you need God's confirmation. Don't do anything unless you have it." □

During that unforgettable week three people came to talk to Nancy, each one offering unsolicited counsel. First came a fellow who had prayed over Tye in one of the meetings. He didn't know who Tye was married to, and he didn't know exactly what the issues were. Still, he felt compelled to seek Nancy out, so he watched Tye to see who he was with. Once he found her, he said to Nancy, "I feel God has something in store for you in your marriage, and you need to stay with your husband. You're going to do great things together in ministry."

The second person was a counselor Nancy had gone to see during the conference. Days after their session he called her aside. "I believe that God has some great things in store for you and your husband," he volunteered.

The third suggestion came in the form of a prayer time in the women's support group. It was just one word. And the word was *love.*

Nancy thought, *OK, God, if this means what it sounds like it means, I need to stay. If so, I'll obey you.*

After the conference, when the Gameys returned to their responsibilities in Winnipeg, both Tye and Nancy knew that if she was to remain in the marriage, things had to change. They weren't quite sure what, but they both realized that they needed to start sharing their thoughts and feelings on a totally different level than they ever had before. And Tye needed to have an accountability process set with someone.

At the time Tye worked at a gospel mission for street people. He felt his boss needed to know what was going on, but he was afraid of the consequences. He nervously told Nancy, "If I tell him, I may lose my job."

"If you lose your job," Nancy countered, "then God will just have to look after us. I believe you need to do this as a step of obedience."

A New Kind of Intimacy

For Tye and Nancy, the months that followed the Exodus conference in 1990 became a period of intense reconstruction. They went through many months of celibacy as more issues related to Tye's sexual abuse surfaced. Nancy had to learn by experience that sex was not the most important sign of love. Together the two learned to define intimacy in an expanded way, including deepened honesty in communication and understanding.

Tye came to see that his past sexual abuse had caused him to question whether he was lovable for anything other than sex. The period of celibacy he and Nancy shared helped him overcome that lie. Likewise, Nancy had to realize that sex was not the answer to Tye's deepest needs.

During that year another pattern became evident. In the past Tye had often resisted when Nancy took the initiative in anything, yet he had been unwilling to make the first move on his own. The two of them had to work on this issue. Specifically, Tye had to take more responsibility for his accountability. And Nancy had to let him.

Tye describes that turbulent period of time:

Even though I was in the midst of struggling and we were really hurting, Nancy and I were still thinking about getting involved in ministry. We knew that God was taking us through all this for a purpose. We had always been committed to full-time ministry. It was just something that God had laid upon our hearts. And now, as God started to deal more specifically with my homosexuality, my gender identity issues and our marriage relationship, I knew that there were so many other men and women out there who were looking for the same answers we needed.

I can remember at times, when I was active in homosexuality, sitting in a bar or in a home with friends, hearing them say, "I don't want to be this way my whole life, but what can we do? Where do we go? Who do we talk to?"

The only message we'd ever heard was that this is who we were and that there was nothing that could be done about it. I realized that it was only by the gift of the Holy Spirit in my life that he had continued to stir the hope that change was indeed possible.

So that's why I wanted to get involved in ministry. I wanted to be able to share, to give back to others what I had received from so many wonderful people. □

God answered Tye's prayers when Tye became director of New Direction for Life, an ex-gay ministry in Winnipeg, Manitoba. That was eight years ago, and for Tye, it amounts to the most fulfilling thing he has ever done in his life. He wouldn't want to be doing anything else. When people ask him, "What keeps you going? Why do you keep doing this?" Tye just smiles. He has a deep passion to minister to those who are stumbling along the same rough, rocky and lonely road that he has traveled.

Together the Gameys affirm without hesitation that their battle with Tye's homosexuality has allowed them to experience the grace of God and his mercy in a way that they couldn't have and wouldn't have otherwise known. For as long as Tye can remember, he has felt that there was something different about himself. It has been through that sense of difference that God has revealed himself to Tye. It is the desire of his heart that people learn they are not alone in their homosexual behavior or gender confusion.

"Nancy and I have survived," he explains. "Our marriage has survived, and our family has survived." And he continues,

That is because of God's grace and God's love. And I truly am thankful

for all he has done. While sometimes when I am tired or stressed I still strug-
gle with lust, weeks will go by when I don't even think homosexual thoughts
or experience temptation. I am in love with Nancy, and I am sexually
attracted to her. God is using the healing we have found to give hope to others.
We thank God for our Christian counselor who believed change was possible.
We are grateful for our supportive church and friends. And we continue to
praise God for the ministry of Exodus International. □

9

"If Only You'd Been a Girl"

Tom Cole

*T*om Cole was the third son in a family of six children, and his mother repeatedly told him that she wished he'd been a girl. Still, despite his arrival as a baby boy and in spite of her insensitive repetition of the disappointment surrounding his birth, Tom's relationship with his mother was always close and warm.

Through Tom's young eyes during the early sixties, his mom was the consummate mother and homemaker. When the six children were very young, late every afternoon she would bathe them, dress them in clean clothes, and send them out to sit on the front porch to wait for their dad and welcome him home from work. To Tom, it was like a scene from *Ozzie and Harriet*—almost surreal.

But none of the family values that manifested themselves in the Cole household contributed to a healthy sense of manhood for young Tom. Beginning with his failure to be born a girl and because of his almost complete estrangement from his father, gender confusion came early to him. Tom had a fair complexion, rosy cheeks and big brown eyes with long eyelashes. He still remembers his mother's unabashed admiration for his beauty. "You'd be such a pretty girl," she'd say with a sweet, affectionate smile.

Such words must have cut deep into Tom's personality. He surely didn't feel much like a "real" boy. And his dad wasn't much help. During Tom's childhood his father worked long hours, and when he would finally arrive at home, he'd simply eat dinner, read the paper and fall asleep. In those early years Tom systematically built a wall between his father and himself. The fact was that they really didn't like each other at all.

And not surprisingly, school was a challenge, which Tom faced with mixed emotions. On the one hand, he loved to learn. On the other, he deeply feared the daily harassment he experienced. One day he came home scraped and beaten, and his father growled, "If you're going to make it in this world, you're going to have to fight."

"But Daddy, I'm afraid to fight."

His father's face flushed with anger. He forced Tom's hands up and started jousting with his fists. Unable or unwilling to respond, Tom stood there and cried. He was already learning to hate his father for forcing him to be something he could never be. The truth was that he despised all males and vowed in his heart that he would never be like them. He recalls:

My lack of interest in contact sports alienated me from the other boys in the neighborhood. When we lined up to pick teams, I would be last and someone would remark, "Oh no, we got stuck with Cole. He's a sissy." Each time I heard those words, my heart grew colder and harder.

As far back as I can remember, I was called names like fag, queer and sissy. My gentle demeanor and compassionate nature, on the other hand, made me compatible with the neighborhood girls; soon they became my sole source of friendship.

One day in fifth grade our teacher tried an experiment in communication. She had the class gather in a circle and talk about the things that bothered them. Suddenly I became the center of the conversation. The boys in the class began to complain, "Cole is a fag. We don't want to sit by him or work on projects with him." When the teacher asked me how I felt about these comments, I ran from the classroom, crying and feeling sick to my stomach. □

As Tom grew older, he and his father clashed more and more frequently. And the more they fought, the more he realized that his mother was the one who really loved him and would always be his staunch defender. During Tom's teen years his mother intervened in one of the fights and took Tom's side. On one occasion her husband told her that someone had to go—either Tom or he would have to leave the house.

"Well, then you'll just have to be the one to go, won't you?" she replied. "In fact, you can go right now." Eventually the problem was resolved, but the sense of being caught in the middle between his parents remained in Tom's heart.

An Important Spiritual Step

Tom's mother was Roman Catholic. She had decided at one point in her life to become a nun and had changed her mind at the last minute, just before taking her vows. Tom's father was agnostic, and his children never heard about his having any sort of a religious upbringing. If he had any faith at all, he kept it to himself.

Except for his father, Tom's family attended the Catholic church. Tom recalls always having had a sense of God and his presence in his life. A lonely child, he sometimes made up songs and sang them to God while he took long walks. He didn't fully understand the concept of who Jesus was, but he knew that God was real. He describes one meaningful experience:

I remember so well when I made my first communion. It was a wonderful day. I got all dressed up, and my mom and I went to church alone. The day before we had picked out a new, starched, white clip-on tie. We bought a rosary and a prayer book too. I felt so special.

As I made my communion, I felt God's presence. Not long after, my mother got into a fight with the parish priest, and we stopped going to church. I think if we had stayed, I might have considered the priesthood. But as I grew older and learned about evolution and humanistic thought at school, I rejected the idea of God. Slowly there was no place for God in my life. Still later on in life, before I returned to Christ, I began to search for meaning through New Age philosophies and Eastern mysticism. □

Playing a "New Game"

When Tom was eight or nine years old, an older boy in the neighborhood began paying an unusual amount of attention to him. Because Tom's relationship with other males was anything but pleasant, the attention was exciting, and Tom was elated about it. One day while the two were playing together, the older boy led Tom into a tent that had been pitched in his backyard. He said with a grin, "I have a new game for us to play." Once they were inside the tent, he began to undress and told Tom to do the same.

While Tom was being sexually molested, he felt fear, revulsion and the intense need to run away. Yet mixed with these negative feelings were sensations of great physical pleasure. After the encounter Tom avoided his friend and buried the incident deep in his memory. Because of his deep shame he told no one that he had been molested.

Instead, when puberty began, Tom began to experiment sexually with other boys in the neighborhood. He and another boy began what turned out to be a six-year physical relationship. Although Tom felt cheapened by these experiences, he was relieved to think that at least he finally had some friends. Somewhere inside, however, he suspected that they only wanted him to provide them with sexual release.

In college Tom majored in music and drama. He joined a vocal jazz ensemble and met a male singer who was out of the closet with his homosexuality. One day Tom asked him if he'd take Tom to a gay bar, and his friend readily agreed. Tom remembers the incident:

I felt fear and excitement as I looked forward to visiting the bar. I was nineteen years old, but most people thought I looked fourteen or fifteen.

When we walked through the door, I immediately noticed that many of the men were staring at me. Even though I felt like an animal on display in the zoo, I also loved the attention. I met a much older man, and we planned a date for the following week. He lavished attention on me, and I was thrilled. But after a few times together he seemed to lose interest in me. The next week I saw him with another guy who looked even younger than I did.

I found it difficult to enter into a long-term relationship with other men. I think the main problem was that deep down we all knew what we needed really couldn't be fulfilled that way. I think what we were after was love and acceptance. Unfortunately, what we ended up getting was nothing much more than selfish sexual gratification. After a while, as I began to see that my relationships weren't lasting, I didn't try for emotional attachment anymore. I sought sexual release, and I became sexually addicted. □

"Don't you think it's a little strange that all we talk about and think about is sex?" Tom asked a group of his gay friends one day. "Is that what the average heterosexual is like?"

No one responded. They stared at Tom and glanced at each other but clearly didn't have an answer. As for Tom, he was beginning to be more and more sure that what they were experiencing really wasn't right. And besides the obsession with sex, another problem was beginning to emerge in the gay community.

Tom came out of the closet in 1980. Back then what is now called AIDS was still known as GRIDS—Gay-Related Immunodeficiency Syndrome. Interestingly, there was very little talk about either GRIDS or AIDS. Men were getting sick and dying all around town, yet there was a heavy blanket of denial thrown across the gay community. They all heard about safe sex, yet no one seemed to be practicing it.

"The truth is," Tom says today, "I was so miserable that I didn't care if I got AIDS and died. That would have simply shortened the pain and torment I lived with. Many of my friends eventually succumbed to the disease. And those of us left behind did nothing to protect ourselves or others from contracting the disease."

One night Tom was shocked to see his younger brother at the club. Tom learned that his brother was involved in a seemingly healthy gay relationship. At the time, he thought, *Maybe it can work after all.* But before long he saw the relationship deteriorate to a violent end, and he lost hope for a long-term gay relationship.

From the age of nineteen until he was around twenty-five, Tom Cole had between three and four hundred sexual partners. At twenty-six, depression set in; he began to drink and use cocaine to deaden the loneliness.

Rosie's Unconditional Love

One night, in total despair, Tom decided to end his life. He swallowed a big handful of painkillers and washed them down with a fifth of vodka. To his dismay, he awoke the next day. He was alive, but he felt as if he had been, as he describes it, "run over by a truck." He was more miserable than ever. He explains what happened next.

Soon after my suicide attempt I met a woman at work named Rosie who talked constantly about having a personal relationship with Jesus Christ.

Rosie Smith is one of the most beautiful Christian women I've ever met. I was a cook in a restaurant, and Rosie was a waitress. Those who've worked in restaurants know that cooks and waitresses usually hate each other. There is an unwritten rule that never shall the two unite in agreement on anything. But with Rosie it was different. She liked the cooks, and the cooks liked her. She was always talking about God and saying things like "Praise the Lord," and telling us about Jesus.

I was an obscene person, constantly making sexual jokes and swearing every other word. But Rosie never told me that the way I talked was wrong. I read New Age books and horror novels, but Rosie never condemned me for that either. I was sexually messed up and would mimic sex acts with the other cooks, but she never pointed out that my homosexuality was wrong. Instead she shared the love of Christ with me.

One night as she was leaving to go home, Rosie said, "My husband and I will be praying for you, Tom."

I was shocked. "You pray for me?"

"Yes," she said. "We pray for you every night." Just as she went out the door, she added, "Tom, I love you. I just want you to know that I love you."

The words ripped my heart open. I knew she was speaking the truth. I knew she loved me. All the years of hurt and pain and hardness were suddenly broken open. The wall I had erected in my heart was blasted down. I began to cry as the realization of what she'd said hit me. I ducked under the counter so she couldn't see me crying. I knew at that moment that whatever it was she had, I wanted it too.

Not long after, I asked Rosie if I could go to church with her. She said that she and her husband would pick me up. I accepted Christ that Sunday. Rosie and her husband, Ron, then took me on as a disciple. They taught me about God and his Son Jesus Christ. They walked with me through difficult times.

They saw me stumble and fall and then watched God pick me back up. They saw me come to Bible study and prayer meetings at their home drunk or high. But through it all they walked with me; they prayed for me; they showed me God's truth in Scripture. I would not be alive today if it weren't for the witness of this beautiful woman in Christ. □

After Tom's commitment to Christ one of his first tasks was to work his way through the process of forgiving those who had hurt him. The first person that came to mind was his father. Realizing that Jesus had instructed his disciples to forgive so that they too would be forgiven, Tom made the decision to forgive his dad for all the problems in the past. As he let go of his bitterness, he didn't feel a tremendous amount of emotion, but he knew that it was a significant moment.

Then, when he talked to his father the next time, he was surprised to feel a surge of love for his dad. From then on, whenever he spoke with him, he said, "I love you, Dad."

"I love you too, son," Tom's dad responded one day. What a joy it was for Tom to hear those words from his father's mouth!

Before long the two men were hugging one another without reluctance.

Not long ago Tom's father attended a church where Tom was sharing his testimony. Naturally, Tom was extremely nervous about his dad hearing his story. Tom's mother died some years ago, and his father's fiancée was with him. Tom couldn't help but notice that they both cried through a good portion of his story.

After the service Tom's father took him in his arms and embraced him for a long time. "I'm so very proud of you, son," he said with tears still flooding his eyes. The words that Tom had longed to hear had finally been spoken.

"My heart broke at the sound of those words," Tom recalls. "I will never forget that day as long as I live."

A Woman Named Donna

Even after his reconciliation with his father, there were still some questions in Tom's mind about what God had in mind for his future. Would he ever find a woman to love, someone who would love him in return? Would he ever be a father? Would he someday have a family of his own, or was that simply too much to hope for?

This caused Tom to reflect upon his childhood and teen years, recalling his responses to the opposite sex.

At a very early age Tom had realized that he didn't look at girls and women the way his male contemporaries did. In fact, he had not been attracted to females at all. When puberty hit, it had become clear to Tom that something was seriously wrong with him. *Charlie's Angels* was the hit television program of the time, and Tom's brothers had posters of the Angels all over the bedroom that the four of them shared. Tom had stared at the posters, hoping to experience something, anything. Nothing had happened.

Instead, when he'd looked at a picture of James Caan, he'd felt a strong attraction and sexual arousal. But who could he have talked to about this strange situation? There was no one with whom he could have trusted his feelings. So he'd kept the confusion to himself and had simply hoped for the best.

In high school Tom had dated a girl who was only interested in a platonic relationship. He'd found out later that she too had suffered a childhood molestation and was afraid of most males. Dating Tom had felt safe to her. So this wounded pair had gone out for three years, throughout high school. Their relationship had provided cover for Tom from the inquisitive prying of those around him and had provided safety for the girl. But beyond friendship, there had been nothing more to the relationship.

Now, even after coming to Christ, Tom didn't experience any change in his attraction toward women. Although his attraction to males had diminished, no feelings for females had replaced it.

Then Tom met a woman named Donna. They got acquainted at a prayer meeting, where the two of them made a quick spiritual connection, and they began a prayer partnership. Donna, a former lesbian, had a clear understanding of Tom's past struggles—she'd had similar struggles of her own. After they had spent two years studying the Bible and praying together, Tom became increasingly aware that his feelings for Donna were more than platonic.

One day Donna arrived at Tom's workplace to pay him a visit. As she came in, for the first time he noticed her well-endowed figure and felt a strong sexual attraction to her. It dawned on him that, at age twenty-six, he was experiencing feelings that most boys go through at puberty. Soon Tom and Donna were dating. Three months later they were married.

The Coles' first year of marriage was torture as insecurities poured out. Tom sought solace in phone sex with men, which simply added to his confusion. Then he heard a broadcast on homosexuality, featuring an interview with Dr. Elizabeth Moberly, a writer and speaker who had done extensive research into the root causes of homosexuality.

It was not until after coming to Christ that Tom had been able to revisit the early molestation he had experienced in the backyard tent. His Christian perspective had also made it possible for him to take an objective look at his family's dynamics—his remote and unapproachable father, his overly involved mother.

Now, as Dr. Moberly spoke about same-gender deficits, Tom realized that he had many close female friends in his life but no significant male friendships. He prayed right then, asking God to send him two men with whom he could share his struggles. The Lord was faithful and sent two men within the next year. They were gentle and compassionate, and they held Tom accountable.

God also sent along another friend. Tom immediately realized that he would have been strongly attracted to this man back in his gay life. Tom was nervous and uneasy as the two of them attended a weekend conference together. Finally, he decided to share his insecurities. "I am really afraid of getting close to other men," Tom said, going on to explain a little about his gender identity issues.

This man responded with wisdom and gentle love. "Just because I've never struggled with homosexuality doesn't mean that I don't fear intimacy," he said in all sincerity. He pointed out that men often talk about weather or sports to avoid discussing their feelings and what is really happening in their lives. Tom felt both surprised and relieved by his new friend's words.

Little by little Tom was learning that he could, in fact, be intimate with a man without being sexual with him. And for the last seven years he has also experienced attractions to other women besides Donna. For some men, that might be a problem; for Tom Cole, it is a sign of health.

Passing Along the Blessings

When Donna gave birth to the Coles' first child, Tom was overwhelmed with both joy and worry. He pleaded with God, "How do I raise a son?"

Tom almost instantly sensed the Lord's response in his heart: "Just love him."

Today little Isaac Cole is all boy. Shortly after his birth another son came along, followed by two daughters. As with most parents, the children are among Tom and Donna's greatest joys.

As Tom and Donna continued to find freedom from their gay

past, they began to minister to others seeking the same hope and healing. Then they joined the board of directors of Reconciliation, a local Exodus ministry in Detroit. Two years later Tom became Reconciliation's director. Today Tom and Donna's vision is to help Christians who long for change in their homosexual desires.

Tom is sometimes asked what the most important thing is that he can say to those who struggle with homosexuality. He replies, "I tell them that God is no respecter of persons. That if God can heal me, he can heal anyone. I tell them not to lose hope because God is the God of hope. I tell them that in the last eleven years of ministry I have seen God faithfully heal person after person who comes to him with a hungry heart. I also tell them that they can't do it alone. No man is an island. We need one another to help each other through what is usually a difficult, painful and sometimes lengthy process. But God is the God of change." About his present circumstances, Tom writes:

Our marriage has its moments of tension and stress, as do all marriages. But we have grown in our love for one another. Our children are growing up to be responsible citizens, bright home-schooled students and strong Christians. It's wonderful to see them blossom in creativity and personality without the fear of intimidation and harassment that often occurs in the public school system. I delight in my children and thank God every day that he saw fit to bring these four beautiful beings into my care.

Meanwhile, Donna and I continue to share our stories wherever people invite us to speak. We have appeared on Extra, 20/20 *and in the "Families" TV ad about leaving homosexuality that raised a lot of controversy. We share our stories in newspapers, magazines, on radio call-in shows and on the World Wide Web. I believe that God has called me to go into all the world and proclaim what God has done for me. I have yet to refuse to tell my story, and I will continue to share it as long as I have the opportunity. The Bible tells us to "comfort those in any trouble with the comfort we ourselves have received from God" (2 Corinthians 1:3-4). I will do that until my dying breath!* □

10

Finding Love in Action

John Smid

John Smid can easily remember back over two decades to a turning point in his life, a night when he decided to leave his wife and daughters in order to pursue homosexuality.

On that unforgettable night in October 1979 I was anxious, excited and full of curiosity. Opportunity had finally come my way. I had been wrestling with increasing homosexual desires and fantasies for some time, and I had no idea how or where I was going to get satisfaction. But all that was about to change. That night, while I was home taking care of our two young daughters, Mike, a gay man from my work, called me. "John, I'll be at the bar across from your neighborhood. Would you like to come over and talk?"

My wife, Kris, and I rarely went anywhere without each other, and it had never entered my mind to go out at night alone, especially to a bar. I didn't frequent bars or drink alcohol to any great extent. But that particular night Kris had been bowling with friends, and when she returned home, I mentioned

Mike's call. She asked if I was going. I felt her implicit permission, so I made the decision to seize this opportunity. Thinking maybe I could finally break the barrier to my true feelings wide open, I said, "Yes, I think I'll go."

A few minutes later, once I had made myself as comfortable as possible at the bar, I revealed my homosexual struggles to Mike.

Mike's response caught me off-guard. He said, "John, I've known this about you for some time. You know, it's easy to read these things in other homosexuals." His disarming comments drew me into unrestrained conversation. Once the dam burst, I flooded him with questions, discussion and revealed to him my deepest longings. The evening ended up in a homosexual encounter with Mike.

He informed me that there was an entire community of gay men in our area, and he would make sure I got introduced to them. I felt scared, anxious and filled with desire, hoping that my fantasies would finally be fulfilled. My hunger for male connection and attention was at its peak. My entire life took a turn that night. But in the process I had broken my vows of committed marriage. □

Looking for Love

John married Kris when he was nineteen years old. He had gone out with her for a couple of years during high school, and their dating relationship had been a rocky one, with many emotional ups and downs and breakups. John never had a sexual relationship with anyone prior to his marriage, and up until then he had not defined his attractions to men as being homosexual.

He decided when he got married that he no longer had to attend church, so he was not pursuing a life that included spiritual guidance or a relationship with God. The one thing that drew John to Kris was the fact that she had come from a very difficult family background, which was similar to his. In his neediness John thought that if anyone could understand his hurts, maybe she could. He hoped that if they got married he would not have to deal with constant fears of rejection. Perhaps he could find safety in his wife's companionship and a hiding place from his life of pain.

But after they were married, it seemed to John that he could never communicate his needs in a way that Kris could hear and understand. The frustration in their lack of intimacy grew. The deep struggles John had encountered with many of the significant women in his life caused him to have a hard time trusting his wife with his deepest feelings. It may have appeared to outside observers that the Smids' relationship was secure and the perfect example of a good marriage. But that wasn't the case. John describes the situation:

We had been married for several years and were expecting our first child. I was working at a convenience store where I was alone a lot. I used the Play-girl magazines available there to spark my sexual interest. A deep curiosity about men drew me to the male photographic subjects. I started to fantasize more and more about what it would be like to be sexually active with men. This pornography became a significant factor in my homosexual desires taking root.

I was finding great excitement in my new fantasies, but my commitment to marriage was still strong. I had made a vow that I would never divorce my wife and put my children through a family breakdown like the one I had gone through as a child. In this commitment I had decided to try one more way to refresh my marriage. I had always been very conservative in the attention that I gave Kris. My gifts to her always fit in our cash budget, but this time I decided to go against my conservative ways. I was going to go all out in buying her a Christmas gift. I wanted desperately to get her attention and feel as though, for once, I had done something right. □

Kris loved to sew, and for a long time she had wanted a good machine. So John purchased a top quality machine with all the latest bells and whistles, even though he had to resort to time payments in order to purchase it. One day, not long before Christmas, he arrived at home and a distressed Kris met him at the door. "John, this Singer credit card came in the mail today. How did we get this?"

John had no choice but to be honest with her. But his secret had been ruined, and he felt disappointed and sad. Still he didn't give up—not yet. In his determination to please Kris and make her love him more, he thought up another plan.

Microwave ovens had just become popular for common home use. John talked with a number of relatives, asking if they would be willing to give him money toward a gift for Kris instead of buying a gift for him. John told them he wanted to do something very special for Kris that year. He used the relatives' money as a down payment, bought a great oven and put the rest on a sixty-day plan. Soon it was Christmas day, and he was full of excitement about his surprise.

After all the gifts were opened, he said, "Wait! I have one more gift. Kris, close your eyes."

When Kris ripped open the big box, she didn't seem surprised at all. Minutes later John found out that she had seen the bill for the gift, and once again she had known about his plan.

John recalls that he completely shut down that day. He felt that he had done everything he possibly could to cause his wife to love him, and nothing had worked. His reaction to this was to make an inner vow: *I'll never be able to meet the needs of a woman, no matter how hard I try.*

Deep inside John's heart that day was the end of his marriage and the beginning of his separation from Kris. No one knew it, but he began to look for some other source of love to meet his needs.

Broken Marriage, Broken Hearts

John continued to find comfort fantasizing about other men. It wasn't long before fantasy didn't satisfy him, and he wondered what it would be like to be relationally intimate with a man. He hungered for a same-sex relationship that would simulate marriage. Curiously, at the time he knew nothing about homosexuality and had never had an opportunity to talk with anyone about it. He explains:

I'd had a long struggle in my relationship with men. I'd always felt detached from my own masculinity. I had made the decision that if being a man meant that I had to be gruff, mean, shut down and angry, then I didn't want to be one. I wanted nothing to do with that for myself. I had also never felt a sense of belonging in a group of men. This extreme void in my life left me hungry for the acceptance from men, and I thought I could find this in homosexual men. They seemed to be different from straight men.

Once I had my first homosexual encounter with Mike, the man from work, I knew that I could have sex with men the way I had fantasized. I could finally forget trying to satisfy a woman, and I could feel cared for by a man. I could feel safe with others who were like me. I didn't have to be alone. The gay community enabled me to not feel so weird after all. □

Shortly after John's homosexual adultery he told his wife that he wanted a divorce. He felt more driven than ever to fulfill his homosexual desires, and at this point nothing was going to stop him. Many people tried to help, but John refused their advice. His mother-in-law was someone who had always cared about him. In one of their discussions she said, "John, I will never believe you are a homosexual."

"Today," John says, "more than two decades later, I understand her words. But at the time, I was having such intense homosexual thoughts and desires that I couldn't hear her." Instead of affirming John's masculinity, her comments caused him to feel unaffirmed and misunderstood. He ignored her and fought against her desire to help him.

John's dad received much the same response. "Dad, I'm gay," he told his father. "I am going to get a divorce from my wife and get involved in the gay lifestyle."

All John remembers today from that evening's discussion were tears, love and a father who was trying to share wisdom from his own life experience. "John, don't do this. Leaving your family will not help anything. I don't want to see you do this to yourself or to your family."

John's dad didn't scold his son or get angry. But John was stubborn. Again, at that point in his life he wasn't willing to listen to anyone who disagreed with him.

Kris wanted counseling, so John agreed but then found a counselor who would support his homosexuality. He kept that information to himself, scheduled an appointment, and off they went. The only thing this counselor offered was to help them divorce amicably. John also found out about a pastor who he thought would support his new lifestyle, so the Smids went and talked with her. She told Kris that she and John had no options left and that divorce was imminent. "John is gay," she explained to Kris, "and he needs to affirm his homosexuality."

Meanwhile, John was meeting more gay friends and had already had several more sexual encounters. He decided to tell Kris that he was leaving. After talking to one of the men with whom he was having an affair, John was convinced—it was time for him to move on. He remembers that painful day:

Kris chose to take our children and go out for the day, giving me the freedom to pack my things and leave. Just as I finished packing and was about to go, she returned. The picture of my wife and children staring at me while I was deserting them is one I will never forget. I felt as if I was killing them while they were looking right at me. My pain, neediness, rebellion and deep fleshly desires enabled me to find enough denial to just drive away. My decision to pursue homosexuality had destroyed my family. It impacted the lives of Kris and my two daughters forever after.

I tried to convince myself that I was about to find a new life and the new relationships that appeared to be the answer for all my needs. I often said that the piece of the puzzle that had been missing from my life had been found. I was gay! I was happy! I was satisfied!

In reality, I was lost in my brokenness. I was deceived, empty and scared. My first relationship ended when he introduced me to someone I was more attracted to. This began a pattern of sexual encounters and broken relationships. I was empty, hurting and feeling like I had been stripped of all my self-

worth. I didn't think I was going to live through the pain and feelings of rejection. I began to feel like I could understand, at least in part, what Kris might have gone through. All these feelings churning around manifested themselves in suicidal thoughts. □

God's Plan for Deliverance

It wasn't long before John's thoughts of self-destruction were eclipsed by a different idea. "You don't have to live this way any longer," a voice said to John one night in 1982. By then he was twenty-eight years old. He had no idea that such a simple statement, heard in his heart during a church service, would have such a powerful effect on his life.

By this time John had already acknowledged that Jesus was his Savior and that the Bible was true and filled with encouraging words from God. And now, although the words he heard that night were not audible, they were absolutely clear to him. God had just given him the hope he needed in order to face the next two years of his life.

Those two years were filled with relational bankruptcy and extreme discouragement. Despite his trust in God's word, John still did not really understand what God had to say about homosexuality. He still thought that a homosexual relationship with another Christian would be a practical solution to his needs and would be acceptable to God. But no matter what he did or whom he was with, John still had a deep emptiness in his heart that no man could fill. And at the very core of his heart was the greatest fear of all: being alone.

Nonetheless, during Valentine's week in 1984 John made one of the hardest decisions of his life. The true Lover of his soul was asking him to make a choice. He could either choose to go to a Christian singles' retreat that weekend, which was threatening to his partner, or he could continue in his present pattern of relational and sexual addiction. So instead of red roses and romance he began the difficult process of moving away from a three-year relationship.

How did all this come about? John had begun to attend a new

church, one that offered something he had never experienced before. For the first time in his life he found himself relating to men who were loving, sensitive, physically and emotionally affirming, all in a nonsexual context. This church's singles' retreat offered something that John had looked for all his life: a social environment with others that was reflective of his Christian faith. John had been raised in a Catholic home where his father had clearly been sold out to God. But until then John hadn't been able to find a place for himself in church—any church—where he really felt he belonged. At this new church, things were very different. However, John still had some doubts about what he was getting into:

I wondered anxiously, How will I fit in at the retreat? *Fear of all fears:* I have to share a hotel room with three other guys. What if they find out that I'm coming away from a homosexual relationship?

During my first night in a double bed with one of them, I felt like a mummy wrapped up in a bundle of insecurities. I did not sleep a wink for fear that I might bump into my bedmate in my sleep.

God was incredibly gracious to me that weekend. I had never experienced so much encouragement and excitement without the guilt of sin in my life. But after the retreat, things got a little rocky and I felt compelled to call my former partner. As I had done many times in the past, I manipulated him into coming over to my house. I fell into my old pattern, and we had a sexual encounter.

What would I do now? I had just violated my new life. How would my pastor respond if I told him about my homosexuality? I made an appointment with Dennis, the singles' pastor. Sitting in his office I told him the whole truth without mincing any words. With a suspicious mind I was testing him with my story.

Pastor Dennis looked at me with compassion and made one statement that still stands out to me: "John, you're right. Homosexuality is wrong." He read a biblical passage from Romans, then told me he'd stand beside me and work with me to help me see my way clear of this sin. There was no judgment, no fear, just commitment. That was all I needed at the time. I wanted so much to be accepted in this strange and mysterious world of "straight" men. His words felt like life-giving water to my parched, thirsty soul. □

After that conversation with Dennis, John never fell into homosexual acts again. Within a few weeks he found a small group of church friends who loved him and wanted him in their lives. At long last, he had found a place of belonging, a placed he'd always longed for. His new friends—Clark, Debbie, Dawna, George and others—quickly became his life-support system. He told them about his past life and his struggle with homosexuality. Although they were stunned at first, they all stood with him, just as his pastor had done. Not one person rejected John because of his past. He recalls the early days of his new life:

God knew I needed to feel like I belonged to this group, so he inspired my pastor to ask me to serve in ministry by emceeing the weekly singles' meetings. After that I became involved as the coordinator of the entire Thursday night ministry. God was giving me a purpose. I had value and gifts. I saw that others could gain from my life, just as I could gain from theirs.

My friend Clark became one vessel God used to bring about a tremendous amount of healing. We spent one night each week just talking. Clark was committed to me; he was not afraid of my past or current struggles. He would confide in me about his own past. Clark could talk about anything without embarrassment and always keeping in line with God's truth. He was confident in his own masculinity so my homosexual issues did not threaten him. □

Day after day, week after week, God surrounded John with healthy relationships. He and a friend named George spent time together. George was interested in knowing John. He asked meaningful questions and dug into John's life, helping him process unexplored feelings and negative thoughts that had built up over the years.

Debbie, Dawna and other women became John's sisters in the Lord. They genuinely liked him and enjoyed having him around. Never once was he ridiculed or teased the way he had been mocked in the earlier years of his life. Genuine healing had begun.

Finding Answers to Life's Toughest Questions

Although by now John had attained sexual abstinence, he realized that he wasn't looking forward to a life of celibacy. He wanted to find a special person with whom he could spend his future, and he started considering the possibility of another marriage. As the idea grew on him, he promised himself that this time he wanted to do it the right way. He prayed about it, and he could see that God was leading him and providing wisdom so that he could eventually live out his vision of a godly, lifelong relationship. John describes what came next:

As I was spending time with several women, one gal began paying special attention to me. Vileen would come to my house to watch me do my yard work. How romantic! I finally recognized her "mating call" and began to get to know her better. I invited her to spend an evening with my two daughters from my first marriage and me. It went very well and so did our first months of the relationship. We were growing very close.

All of a sudden, bam! An emotionally paralyzing wall dropped between us. Oh boy, not again, *I thought.* I'm hurting someone all over again. I didn't expect this as a Christian. I thought my life was all right now. I was feeling frightened and shutting down from our relationship. I told Vileen that I needed help. But where would I get it?* □

Meanwhile, an acquaintance confided in John about his own homosexual struggle. He was still stumbling too often and had no idea how to find victory over temptation. What could John tell him? John immediately realized that he had no answers beyond his personal experience. He had now been free from sexual immorality for almost two years, but he still did not know anyone else who had come from a homosexual background. He had never heard a single testimony from anyone who had found freedom from homosexuality.

Finally, through the national radio show *Focus on the Family,* John found out about ex-gay ministries. He wrote to Love In Action and Exodus International, seeking advice on what to tell his friend. Love In Action responded with an invitation to come to their ministry and serve in their live-in program. John saw this as God's direct answer to his still unspoken desires and dreams. Perhaps in a setting like that he could find out more about the barriers that lay between Vileen and him, as well as learn how to provide answers for other men needing help. John was really excited. How faithful God was to allow him to serve in his kingdom!

John's first weeks with Love In Action turned out to be an uphill climb. He quickly found out that the time had come for him to face up to the real roots of his struggle. But the hard work proved to be worthwhile. In the process God set him free from the many fears and anxieties he had about life. Best of all, John married Vileen in 1988.

Not surprisingly, marriage was by no means the end of John's battle. In fact, marriage was a whole new battleground, which required relevant information about hope and healing. Now that John was more aware of his feelings, being in a close relationship with a woman brought up all his opposite-sex issues. Although he had pretty much resolved his same-sex issues, other problems were buried in his heart. Until then John had not even suspected that they were there.

As he tried to interact with his new wife, hurts, rejections and difficulties of his past relationships with women bubbled to the surface. It wasn't long before he realized that he was feeling a deep-seated anger toward Vileen—an anger that he didn't understand. His critical attitude toward her was unfounded and did not reflect anything she had done. She was kind, considerate and loving. She was not doing anything that would merit his harsh responses. Where was this coming from?

John began to learn about the importance of healing past hurts.

He found anger and pain that had been inside him since his experiences as a two-year-old child, when he had spent a year away from his parents. That little child had felt intense hurt because he'd perceived that his parents had abandoned him. His foster home was loving and caring, but where were his mom and dad? Feelings of rejection brought about by those early family struggles had carried him into a life filled with disappointing relationships. This unexpected awareness helped John to see where his anger toward Vileen had originated. It also cast new light upon his gender confusion and homosexual attractions.

To others who struggle, John has this to say:

Healing from the causes of homosexuality takes time. A relational problem needs a relational solution. The people God has used in my life are too numerous to count. Success, failure and disappointments are all part of the necessary struggles to find a deeper resolution of my homosexual struggles.

Where am I today? I have a loving, committed marriage. I enjoyed a restored relationship with my father before he passed away. I continue to work toward a healthier relationship with my mother. I feel of great value to the Lord and his work. I have a sense of belonging, personhood and relationship with others. At the same time my choice to abandon my home and divorce my wife brought immense pain into her life and the lives of my children that continues even today. Homosexuality is a part of my emotional, physical and spiritual history. It will not be erased as though it never existed. I may still envy a guy who I think is better looking than I am. I still shut down with my wife at times. I periodically have sexual thoughts toward a man.

"So then, what is victory?" you might ask. In my opinion, victory is being able to partake of the fruit of the land that God offers in obedience to his Word. I no longer see homosexuality as an option or desire for my life. I want nothing to do with it. I embrace my God-given relationships too much to destroy them. I embrace my wife and marriage too much to lose it to some momentary empty pleasure. I have developed a cherished relationship with God that I want nothing to destroy.

I can assure you that there is hope, victory and true love in Christ. □

11

From Rage
to Renewal

Pat Allan Lawrence

From an early age Pat Allan sensed the hand of God on her life. She grew up as a missionary kid—a childhood experience that often proves itself treacherous, even in the best of times. She still vividly remembers accepting Jesus into her heart as a five-year-old child in Guyana, South America. That experience was significant to her, but it was soon eclipsed by a series of difficulties that eventually led her away from her early faith.

The Protestant denomination Pat grew up in was conservative—more conservative than her parents, who belonged to it. She often heard during her formative years that the proper role of a woman was to be in the home, cooking and cleaning. A man's place was outside, earning a living, fishing, working on cars and taking care of business.

Pat felt early on that there must be something wrong with her. She really didn't like doing what the church leadership proclaimed that women should do. When she was taught that the role of women was to be submissive, Pat interpreted that idea to mean "being a doormat." And that was a far cry from her naturally engaging and assertive personality. Pat loved her parents and felt particularly close to her father. However, when she was six, something very dark and painful came between them. Pat remembers:

One day in a grocery store, a man came up and began molesting me. He knelt down next to me and sexually abused me. I had no idea what was going on. But as my dad and I were walking out to the car, I told him what had happened, and he got angry. He went back into the store, looking for the man who had molested me, but he couldn't find him.

On the drive home my father didn't explain that he was angry at the other man. I assumed that he was angry with me. That must have been really wrong, *I told myself.* I must have displeased Daddy.

I think from that day on, I began rejecting men. □

About this same time in her life Pat overheard her father telling her mother that he had a hard time picking Patty up and holding her because she was overweight. The little girl, of course, interpreted that as *There is something wrong with me.*

Compounding the situation, not long afterward Pat overheard her father talking to her mother again. "I have a hard time loving Patty," he explained. "I see all my bad qualities in her." Although she knew that her father loved her, after that she never felt that he loved her quite as much as he loved her two younger sisters.

One Tragedy After Another

By the time Pat reached adolescence, the family had moved back to Canada—again. It was bad enough that they moved around a lot, but Pat has come to see that their missionary lifestyle didn't allow her to develop a security in her own identity. She would make new friends, then suddenly she'd have to leave them behind—yet another loss to grieve.

But the family's returns to Canada took place because of even more hurtful conditions. Pat's father had struggled with adultery throughout his years of missionary service. His affairs not only betrayed Pat's trust in her father but came between her and her mother. She explains:

I can remember being in Guyana, always trying to protect Mom, trying to hide my sisters' problems away from her in order to keep her happy. Then when we returned to Canada, I was a typical kid, always arguing with Mom. One day she started to cry, and she spilled out to me the story of Dad's latest affair. That enforced my idea that I had to look after her instead of her looking after me.

I didn't want to be like my mother. I remember making a vow to myself about that. In my mind she kept "allowing" him to have affairs because she kept forgiving him. Today my dad will acknowledge how my mother held the family together, but at that point, I saw it differently. His last affair occurred decades ago. I was with my mother when he was trying to decide whether to stay with Mom or go with his girlfriend. I was so mad at Mom because she hadn't given him an ultimatum.

There was no way that I was going to have a man in my life, if this was what it meant. □

For Pat, things went from bad to worse. At age fourteen, when she was more or less friendless, overweight and struggling with adolescence, an older cousin, who had drawn her to himself as a friend, raped her. In the very midst of the episode this man, whom she loved almost as much as she loved her father, said, "You're fat and ugly, and no man will ever want you."

In a bizarre twist his wife—who had been present during the entire incident—held Pat in her arms afterward. "I feel close to you," she said soothingly, "and I love you. I think you're very beautiful." This incestuous event began to attract Pat to a lesbian perspective. In the days and weeks that followed, Pat started to masturbate obsessively, and though she tried to stop, even repenting in tears before God, she couldn't control the urge. It kept happening.

The longer this struggle continued, the worse Pat felt about herself. *I'm not repentant,* she thought, *so I'd better stop talking to God. He doesn't love me anymore.* Her prayer life soon dried up.

Eventually she went to see her pastor. "How are you doing, Patty?" he asked cheerfully.

"Do you really want to know?" All at once she exploded. Angry words poured out. "I'm doing awful. I—I hate this church—and everything about it!"

The pastor was, of course, taken aback. But rather than calming Pat down and trying to determine what might have ignited such an outburst, instead he gave her a lecture. "You should be ashamed of yourself! You have good parents and a church that teaches the Bible."

After a few minutes Pat had heard more than enough. "I know all that," she shouted, glaring at the man and jumping up to leave. "Goodbye. And don't expect to see me again. I'm never coming back!"

Leaving God Behind

Pat went home and told her father that she was walking away from God. Rather than expressing shock or disapproval, he simply said, "Patty, may I pray with you?" She nodded silently.

"Lord," he prayed, "I ask that you take everything Pat does and turn it to ashes until she makes you the Lord of her life!"

Pat was stunned. She had to believe that God wasn't listening anyway. But she knew that her dad was a praying man. And she knew that he cared and that he wanted the best for her. So despite its very grim implications Pat somehow wasn't offended by her father's prayer. She could only hope that it never got past the ceiling.

It wasn't long before Pat dropped out of high school. And, perhaps at least in part because of her father's prayer, her life actually did begin to fall apart. She continued to struggle with masturbation and intense sexual urges.

I moved out on my own. I met a number of non-Christians and got involved in drugs. I started my own business selling vacuum cleaners. I met Karen, and we decided to become roommates; I didn't know at the time that she was gay. She kept trying to set me up with men, but I kept throwing them out. Finally she asked me, "Do you want to go out with me?"

I responded, "Yes, if you'll take me to a gay bar."

Later she told me that she ran in ahead of me and told everyone to pretend that they didn't know her. She didn't want me to know quite yet that she was gay. But I had already figured it out, and I had decided that I wanted to get involved with her. That night in the bar we were dancing, and I realized that I was enjoying it.

No wonder I feel the way I do, *I told myself. The pieces of the puzzle seemed to fall together in my mind:* I must be gay. That's why I feel so different from other women. *Until that point I didn't have the vocabulary to express what I had been feeling. Now I did. We got sexually involved that night for the first time.* □

Pat tried to establish a "proper" relationship with Karen—one that fit the Christian standards she'd always known. For example, she tried to be faithful to Karen, just as she might have done in a heterosexual marriage.

"Karen, I love you," Pat told her partner one night. In response Karen slapped Pat's face. Pat said it again, and once more Karen stung her with an angry blow. Karen could not receive Pat's love, and her violent reaction was a foretaste of what lay ahead in their wild and destructive relationship.

Before long Pat found out that Karen was fooling around with other women, and she started to do the same. Meanwhile, her alcohol consumption increased, and she began to use heavier drugs. Not surprisingly, the women's domestic violence increased. On one occasion Pat picked up a knife and threatened to kill Karen. On another she threw Karen into a mirror, and it shattered, showering the room with shards of glass.

Pat, by then, was getting into fights with men in bars, as well as having affairs with other lesbians. *If Karen can do it to me,* she decided, *I'll hurt her back.*

The couple broke up several times, but Karen always pleaded with Pat to come back. Pat began to realize that she was actually the stronger of the two. She always knew she could make it on her own, but Karen repeatedly implored that she was unable to function without Pat. Pat remembers her own physical appearance during those days:

I was skinnier when I was with Karen, but that was because of all the drugs I was taking. After I left her, all the weight came back on.

I was always a classy dresser. My style wasn't masculine, but my behavior certainly was. I guess I saw myself as a real-life Xena—beautiful and feminine but fully able to break anyone's neck. I could fight three or four men at a time—no problem. I was also very hard looking; I had purple hair and always wore lots of makeup. □

Meanwhile, the drugs, alcohol and violence were taking their toll on Pat's mind. Sometimes she got into bar fights with men, and afterward she could not remember anything about what had happened.

One time Karen found Pat bleeding and unconscious in the middle of a parking lot. "If you don't smarten up, you can leave," she warned Pat later on that night.

But Pat carried on anyway, playing the sordid cat and mouse game that defined the flawed relationship. When they were in a bar, Pat ignored Karen and flirted with other women. Jealous and insecure, Karen hung around Pat all evening, making sure nothing happened. For the moment, Pat thought she had Karen right where she wanted her. In the meantime, straight men looking for a chance to have a "little fun" sometimes came into the bars. If one of these men so much as asked Pat to dance, her deep hatred of males surged and spewed forth in torrents of words and acts of violence.

Once, after Pat and Karen broke up, Pat moved back home with her parents. One evening she tried to commit suicide.

My parents had left at six o'clock to go out for the evening. I swallowed some pills and went to bed. The next morning my mother found the empty pill bottle in the garbage and ran to my room. She and Dad rushed me to the hospital.

Twelve hours after I'd taken the pills, the concentration of drugs in my body was still above the lethal level. "It's only a miracle that you're alive," the doctor told me later.

Miracle or not, I wasn't happy. "God, I just want to die," I screamed. "You won't even let me do that!"

I was soon back to my old ways, living with Karen, hanging around lesbian bars and taking acid. No one understands what I'm going through, *I thought.* If anyone does, they're as stoned as I am and don't care. □

By then the relationship was doomed. During a separation Pat went to stay with a straight girlfriend who was estranged from her husband. This friend was very understanding because they were both grieving over their broken relationships. One evening they talked about God's unconditional love. Pat's friend, a new Christian, encouraged Pat to talk to God about her messed-up life. "Pat," she suggested, "why don't you just go to God and see what he can do for you?"

Moving Mountains

Pat nodded and thought the matter over. What did she have to lose? She took a deep breath and prayed, "Lord, I love my girlfriends, and I love the drinking and partying. If you want me, you'll have to take me just the way I am. But—please—don't allow me to stay this way."

She paused, thought for a few moments, then continued. "But if you take me, I don't want to be a Christian who just keeps a pew warm. I want to move mountains! In any case, if you want me, you can have me."

Then I saw a picture in my mind. I was down in a pit, with chains and filth all over me. And Jesus was there. But he wasn't standing over the pit saying, "Come on, I'll help you up." He came down into that pit, threw his arms around me and said, "Patty, all I've ever wanted was you. I love you for who you are."

That was more than twenty years ago, and my life has never been the same since. □

Before long Pat's friend had reconciled with her husband, and Pat moved back in with her parents. About six months later she was sitting on her parents' couch. It was New Year's Eve. She had sat there every day for a week, looking out the window and trembling all over.

"Pat, what on earth is wrong with you?" her mother finally asked.

"I'm not sure," Pat's said. "All I know is that God and Satan are fighting in me. My body is the battleground, and I don't know who's going to win."

Unbeknownst to Pat's mother, Karen had asked Pat to move back with her.

God, Pat screamed inside, *I need a miracle!* After this sudden prayer for help, she gave in to temptation and headed for Karen's apartment.

"Hi," she said to Karen, walking in the front door. "I've come back."

To her amazement, her atheist lover scowled at her. "You love your God too much. Get out of here!" Pat instantly knew that God really had answered her desperate prayer. For Karen to send her away was, most certainly, a miracle.

Pat went back home and within minutes the phone rang. It was her pastor returning a call she'd made earlier to the church. "Pat, you asked if you could sing at church tomorrow? Yes, that would be fine. We'll look forward to seeing you then."

Pat hung up, and the phone rang again. It was Karen. "I'm sorry, Pat. Please come back."

But in that short time the path of Pat's life journey had made a radical turn. "It's too late now," she told Karen. "Our relationship is finished."

The new year began with Pat singing a solo in her church about God's wonderful grace. That day—January 1, 1980—became the beginning of Pat's new life in Christ.

A Time and Place for Healing

Due to her erratic relationship with Karen, Pat had recently lost her job. Now she heard about an opening with the Inter-Varsity Christian Fellowship office in Toronto. She went to interview and was hired. After working for several months she took her boss out for lunch. Karen was beginning to phone her at work, and one day she had even sent roses. Pat wanted her boss to know about her background, an issue she hadn't raised at her job interview.

"Pat," he said, "when I interviewed you, I knew there was something you weren't telling me, but God stopped me from asking." He promised Pat that the Inter-Varsity team would stand beside her in dealing with Karen.

Working at IVCF was a time of healing, as I learned to relate to other Christians, basking in their friendship and acceptance. Even in the midst of all my worst fears I prayed that I would love God enough to risk loving other people.

I needed to have individuals who came to me and said, "Hey, you know, I don't like what you're struggling with, but you can come and talk to me anyway."

I had girlfriends who gave me an open door to talk about other women that

I was attracted to. Now that didn't mean they were saying, "No problem—it's OK to go on out and date them." But they gave me the freedom to talk about my struggle so that Satan didn't have as big a grip on me.

I always like to emphasize that before you can get interested in the opposite sex, you need to be able to relate to your own sex. Once a female friend or two said to me that they were willing to work through my problems with me, I could say, "Hey, you know, Satan, you just don't have it!" ☐

Pat's new Christian friends also helped her see that her particular area of sin wasn't any greater than anyone else's. "We've struggled with sexuality too," they explained. "Just not with *homo*sexuality." They put their own battles with celibacy and purity on the same level as hers.

"Many times people involved in homosexuality believe that their sins are the greatest," Pat says, "that nobody else's failures could possibly be as bad as theirs. Their self-pity and shame invariably make their situation worse than it already is." Pat says today that it was a great help to her when her friends helped her find a way to laugh at herself. She learned from them that all Christians are in a growth process. "We really have no choice but to help each other along."

Pat affirms today that the church was a place of help and healing for her. "Fellow Christians have life to give to the individuals struggling with homosexuality, and we can help them grow. For some of them, it's going to take a long time. For others, it won't take so long."

"God works differently in each person's life," she says. "And he uses other believers to do his most essential work. He's not going to bypass using people, because he created us to help one another."

Eventually I went to Ontario Bible College. I met a man who was instrumental in teaching me how to trust men. Peter was a student about my age, and when I first met him, I thought he was stuck-up and totally self-centered; I wanted nothing to do with him.

But before long I felt that God told me to be his friend. One time he took me to a wedding, but he hardly talked to me all day. Later I asked him, "Were you embarrassed to be with me because I'm fat?"

"Yes," he replied.

Believe it or not, I wasn't offended; I knew he was telling the truth, and I respected his honesty. We're still friends today. Through Peter, the Lord has showed me that I could trust at least one man—this particular man—because he was willing to tell the truth.

Peter helped me start saying, "I want to learn how to be friends with men."

In the meantime my counselor was teaching me that I could not generalize the character of all men because of my bad experience with two significant men. Gradually my rage dissipated. As time passed, I learned to go out and simply have fun with men. With God's help and the help of the people he put into my life, I was finally able to overcome my bitter feelings toward males and to actually enjoy them. It was a new experience for me. ☐

After graduating from seminary in 1985 Pat was approached by three different missions to go overseas, but she only had one real burden in her heart: she deeply wanted to minister to homosexuals.

To Love and Be Loved
She threw out a fleece: "Lord, if you want me to stay in Toronto, bring one person into my life who is gay." The next week her sister told her that someone in an ex-gay ministry had preached in her church. Pat telephoned the speaker, and he invited her to his group. Ten days after her prayer she was sitting in a room surrounded by twelve people coming out of homosexuality.

The leader was planning on going overseas, and Pat soon took over the group. A Baptist church in downtown Toronto donated office space, and before long she was putting together a ministry board. Since then God has powerfully blessed the work of New Direction for Life, a ministry to those who seek to change their homosexuality.

Another profound change has also taken place in Pat's life. She recently married Gary Lawrence, and she sees her marriage as a remarkable gift from God.

Although there's still more healing to be done in my life, God has already done miracles. I don't struggle with homosexuality anymore. I'm much more in touch with my feelings. And I am loved. I know my husband loves me. The day we were married, as Gary and I were signing our marriage registration form, he bent down and whispered to me, "You are such a beautiful bride!" God used that moment to sweep away the last vestiges of betrayal, of feeling "less than" because of my weight and of assuming I would always be rejected.

My response to God's amazing grace is to be obedient before him and to do my best. God will do the rest. Whatever the future brings, it's reassuring to know I'm in his hands. I've been a lot of places. And believe me, there's nowhere in the world that I would rather be than with him. How I thank God for all he's done for me. □

12

More Precious Than Gold

Penny Dalton

*P*enny was three months old when her father left for World War II and three and a half years old when he returned. At his homecoming she stood at the top of the stairs—leaning over the railing as he entered the foyer below—and said, "Hi, Daddy! Are you my daddy?"

Emotional distance epitomized the relationship that existed between father and daughter for most of Penny's life. As a result, for many years a sense of misogyny caused Penny to view other females through a warped lens. Thankfully, before the story was completely finished, God stepped in and transformed Penny and ultimately her entire family.

Penny was the oldest of three children, four years between each of them. Their father traveled a great deal and was home only on weekends. As far as the children were concerned, this was just as well because they were afraid when he came home. He was strict, emotionally removed from both his wife and children, bitterly sarcastic and, at times, violent. Although he enjoyed pursuing females, which led to extramarital affairs, he really was a misogynist.

Penny recalls:

I remember when I was around eleven or twelve that my father initiated conversations that were difficult for me. They were filled with subtle sexual innuendoes that made me uncomfortable. As time went on, deeper discussions and questions that I never thought of were being answered for my innocent mind. Sexual advances started gradually. Later came verbal and physical "instructions" of what sex was all about.

No intercourse ever took place, yet there was some physical involvement. I was afraid of Dad, so I wouldn't speak up against what he was doing. Meanwhile, I was angry at my mom. Where was she? Why couldn't she figure out what Dad was doing to me? Who could help me? I felt so violated, both emotionally and physically, that I couldn't stand looking at Dad or even being in the same room with him.

I remember as a young teenager that I was uncomfortable having my girlfriends visit my home. Dad was a terrible flirt, and I felt that my friends were in danger of his advances. One of my friends told me that my dad made a pass at her, and I was sick in my heart, embarrassed, and hated my father for violating my friend verbally. I was so ashamed of him that I couldn't trust him around my friends. I stopped asking anyone over. I hated my father, both for what he was and for what he did. □

Same-Sex Attractions

During third grade Penny was emotionally attracted to her female teacher. She was starved for attention and would do anything to catch her teacher's eye. At ten or eleven years old the same kind of attraction took place with her choir teacher. In Penny's eyes she was the most beautiful woman in the world, and Penny's thoughts were obsessively focused on her.

The choir teacher lived close to Penny's house and occasionally Penny rode to choir practice with her. The child was struck dumb, hardly able to breathe. Just to see the teacher was wonderful, but to be in the same car with her was overwhelming.

As months turned into years, Penny searched deeply into the eyes of the girls she knew, older girls and even the mothers of her friends, yearning for connection. Her soul seemed starved to be seen, recognized and acknowledged. All this hunger for attention was eroticized during puberty. By then she was openly flirting with her girlfriends, and at times she experimented sexually with them.

Penny's gender confusion was compounded by the fact that she had crushes on boys as well as girls. She was puzzled by the feelings that she had for each gender, which seemed to be very different. In her teen years the emotional and sexual attachment to girls seemed safer because she felt no fear of pregnancy. During the late fifties men and women weren't likely to sleep together openly, and fear of becoming an unwed mother was a very real aspect of sexual pleasure.

But there was another difference in her attraction to girls — Penny welcomed pursuit from them. She was quite capable of being flattered by a boy's attention, especially if she liked him, but if he got too close, she recoiled from what felt like aggression. With girls, she thrived on and longed for that same level of attention.

At first Penny was determined not to live a lesbian life. She was sure she would eventually get married and have a family. After years of experimentation, at age twenty-three she was introduced to the gay community of the late sixties. There she learned from her new friends that the straight world was not to be trusted because they "don't understand what we are all about." It was during those years that Penny accepted the fact that she was, after all, a lesbian.

The gay community was affirming for her. She was never uncomfortable with her gender as a woman. She did not hate her femininity. She later discovered that she hated certain types of women (weak, insecure) but she never wanted to be masculine in her role or take on that identity.

I was detached from Mom, hated Dad, and wanted to hurt them both. So I felt justified in doing whatever I wanted—including the pursuit of a lesbian relationship. The first one lasted nine years. In that time I drank heavily and also took recreational drugs. I knew something was wrong, but my emotions were so buried that I couldn't feel anything but emptiness.

For eight years I had been a flight attendant for a major airline while living in New York City. My relationship with my lover was fragmented, and I found myself having an affair with someone on the West Coast that I would see on my layovers in Los Angeles.

My heart was so hard. My spirit was lifeless. I felt guilty about cheating on my lover. But my emotions were so blocked that I rarely spoke of my past sexual abuse. Instead I escaped into heavy alcohol and marijuana use every time I went to Los Angeles. □

One day while Penny was rushing through the airport, a stranger smiled at her. Rage surged through her. What were some people so happy about that they could smile easily and effortlessly? She was resentful of anyone who was simply enjoying life. She was depressed and angry—especially angry—all the time.

Sometimes Penny saw new mothers on a flight, cherishing their brand new babies. She knew all too well that something was wrong with her emotionally because her own heart was stone cold. She had no emotion regarding a precious new life. No feelings of joy arose within her. She was out of touch with reality, but, at the same time, she knew it.

The Breaking Point

Penny could recall times from childhood when she had been emotionally free to feel and express herself before the verbal and sexual abuse began. But now, little by little, a deep fear was chilling her soul. It was abnormal to have no feelings but fear. She had grown incapable of experiencing either joy or love. She was aware of nothing but a deep, frightening emptiness.

On one of her flights to Los Angeles, during which she hoped to see her new lover, Penny felt intense physical pain in her body. She ached all over and was unable to sleep. During her return flight to New York she fell apart. Besides the tremendous pain, she began to hallucinate. She describes the experience:

I was so incapacitated that the other flight attendants sent me up to the cockpit for awhile just to get me out of the cabin. While I was in the cockpit talking to the flight crew, I really flipped. I actually felt like my head was turning around 360 degrees. I was so frightened.

This demonic activity was brought on by an emotional breakdown as well as by drug influence. I panicked. I couldn't control what was happening. I left the cockpit and went into one of the lavatories and tried to throw up whatever this evil thing was within me.

I had always instinctively recognized the need to stay away from occult activities and to never explore them. I had never deliberately opened myself up to the demonic realm. Yet whatever I was dealing with was demonic in nature. I recognized that clearly, even though I was not yet a Christian.

Meanwhile, I invited a man from my flight to come home with me to my apartment. Why would I experience a heterosexual attraction during this time? Fortunately my estranged lover whom I lived with came home, and this stranger fled with his coat, unlike Joseph who left his cloak behind in fleeing sin (Genesis 39:12). □

That night was both sleepless and fraught with physical pain. The next morning Penny was admitted to a psychiatric hospital. She stayed there for six weeks while her baffled physicians struggled to find the correct medication and diagnosis. Some of her behavior during those weeks was so bizarre that she was diagnosed with severe schizophrenia. Three years after her release from the hospital Penny remained heavily medicated, and, although she was able to function, she did so lethargically.

Six months after Penny's discharge from the hospital her lover left her. Raw with emotion and sick with guilt, Penny was newly heartbroken. During this time a lesbian friend began pursuing her. Elaine was in an eighteen-year-long relationship with a woman, and she and Penny and their respective partners had all been friends for years. But now Penny and Elaine became clandestine lovers.

When Elaine's lover found out about the relationship, she threatened to take Penny's life as well as her own, leaving Elaine with the consequences. Sometimes Penny saw her drive past her apartment, well aware that this angry, confused enemy had a gun in her car. Penny and Elaine tried desperately to break up, but in all their despair they were unable to disentangle themselves emotionally.

This time Penny prayed a desperate prayer: "God, what should I do?" She didn't understand her own heart. Did she really love Elaine and want to have a relationship with her, or was she simply enamored with the excitement of having an affair with an older woman who was a gifted artist? Finally Elaine left her lover and signed all possessions over to her. Elaine left the relationship with her art supplies and just enough money for a down payment on a piece of property. The future looked bright with promise.

Born Again—A New Creation

But a year and a half into their new relationship Penny and Elaine were fighting constantly. Their once warm-hearted conversations had frozen over into icy silences. They were drinking heavily—both of them were addicted to alcohol—and they were bored with one another. Penny was reading a lot of books on psychology, trying to change some aspects of her life and searching to understand why she acted certain ways.

But in the midst of the emptiness, during a time when night-mares haunted her nights and emptiness filled her days, God suddenly stepped into Penny's life. She saw Psalms 18:16-17 and 40:2 come to life before her eyes. "He reached down from on high and took hold of me; / he drew me out of deep waters. / He rescued me from my powerful enemy. . . . He lifted me out of the slimy pit, out of the mud and mire."

Penny recalls this unexpected intervention:

The void within me was howling. One morning I awoke and felt an invisible bubble of warm liquid love, which burst into the dark void I was feeling. I somehow knew I could trust the presence of this feeling of love, not fully understanding that it was God's love. I prayed somehow and said that I wanted to get connected to God. I surrendered myself totally over to God.

As a little girl I had been taught about Jesus, and I had always loved God, but I'd never been told that I could know him personally. Even now I didn't think I was searching for God. But God knew I was in need of a relationship with him, and I met Christ in a powerful wonderful way.

What happened to me is recorded in Genesis 1. I am taking liberty to change the wording, but this is how I understand what God did for me that morning. "Now Penny was formless and empty, darkness was over the surface of the deep, and the Spirit of God was hovering over her soul. And God said, 'Let there be light,' and there was light. God saw that the light was good, and he separated the light from the darkness."

Unbeknownst to me, Elaine had had a supernatural encounter with God two weeks before I did. She too had no knowledge of the gospel from the witness of Christians. Elaine had accepted Christ as her Savior just as I had done. God had revealed himself to each of us, without the other knowing. □

At first neither Penny nor Elaine spoke about their separate experiences. But they both began to read the Bible, and God was soon working deeply and swiftly in their hearts. For many years they had been involved in a community of long-term gay couples who shared wonderful homes and a great sense of "family." Suddenly the gay parties at those homes lost their appeal. Dirty jokes were not so easy to listen to. They were changing. What was going on?

Finally the two women began talking a lot about God, and they soon realized that something powerful had happened to them, even though they didn't know what it was. Something very serious was taking place, something life-changing.

"We were born again," Penny explains, still marveling at the experience, "and we didn't even know it."

Before long God led Penny and Elaine to a small, Spirit-filled church where they began to learn about God and who Jesus is. They were taught that when people become Christians, they are made brand new inside (2 Corinthians 5:17). Penny fell deeply in love with Jesus. She was astonished that he would come to her so supernaturally, revealing his love in such a profound way.

For the first time in her life she no longer had a void in her soul. Great peace enveloped her. She was sure, beyond the shadow of a doubt, that she was connected to God through Jesus. A personal God had died on the cross for her. She had believed and received that truth. Now Penny Dalton had new life in him.

New life—what does that mean? What really was happening to me? I wept daily in gratitude because God had come into my heart. I was overwhelmed with an awareness of his wooing me to himself. He moved in. He settled in. He was welcomed in. He was comfortable within.

And as for me, I felt accepted. I felt satisfied. I felt peaceful. I felt forgiven. I felt loved. I was on a honeymoon with Jesus, and I was deliriously joyful. Yet I began to realize that the freedom and release God wanted me to experience in my life were directly connected to my need to look at some difficult areas in my past. Strangely enough, the gay issue was not one of them.

At least not yet . . . □

Not surprisingly, Penny didn't understand forgiveness. She thought that if she forgave her father, she would be reopening all the emotional areas he had violated, that she would be vulnerable again to the old hurts. Eventually she realized that forgiveness doesn't mean agreeing with what others have done to us. Nor does it mean that what they did doesn't matter. Forgiveness, for Penny, meant choosing to release her father from her vengeance. That enabled her to begin removing the hardness from her heart, to start clearing the way toward open communication with the Lord.

This wasn't as easy as it might sound. Penny pleaded with God to give her a new heart for her father. Why? Because even after she had forgiven him, she continued to see pictures in her mind of terrible incidents that had involved him with her. God revealed to Penny that these "instant replays" were Satan's ploy to challenge the Lord's ongoing work in her life.

Penny learned to take authority over her flashbacks. Every time they attempted to haunt her, she commanded in the name of Jesus that they leave. Also, she confessed out loud that she had forgiven her father. It was a real battle, but eventually she experienced freedom from the past.

Beside the whole issue of bad memories, the Lord gave me another clear choice. For years I had grumbled about my dad not having met my needs. Now I sensed God saying, "You had much higher expectations than your father was ever able to fulfill. Are you willing to accept the fact that your father will never be able to meet your needs?"

I was at a point of decision. One path was clinging to my "rights" to hold hatred toward him. Or I could let go of my dream of having a perfect father and allow God to bring healing.

I chose the latter, releasing all my expectations of the perfect father. God would be my Father. I could trust that he would never hurt me. In the instant I made that choice, I felt as though fifty tons had rolled off my back. □

God's Slow, Deep Work

Elaine and Penny didn't know any Christians when they first came to the Lord, but God was working deeply, slowly and thoroughly in their lives without outside help. Through the Holy Spirit's pure influences, the two women longed to do and be everything God was asking of them. In their simple faith they invited God into every area of their relationship—every emotional, spiritual and even sexual area. And, as most Christians know, God will work where he is invited.

God was beginning to bring to Penny truth "in the inner parts" (Psalm 51:6). She was starting to recognize his wisdom and his Word. But she was also trying to ignore the truth that he was

speaking very clearly—about ending her lesbian relationship with
Elaine. Both women knew Christ and wanted him more than anything; yet their hearts were darkened to the fact that their relationship as lovers was sinful. After all, they reasoned, hadn't he known
they were gay when he saved them?

Despite their hesitation the Lord led Penny and Elaine to find
some help. They wanted to meet other gay people who knew Christ
and find out how they dealt with their homosexuality. At first they
went to New York's Metropolitan Community Church. So many of
the gay people there appeared to love God, but Penny and Elaine
had read too much in Scripture to be convinced of the church's
legitimacy.

*The Holy Spirit showed us the false word that was spoken as truth—that
God had created us homosexual and that he would therefore bless our relationship. As much as we wanted to embrace that as truth, we knew too much.
We knew God's love. We had devoured the Bible. We understood the Scriptures
enough to know this was not what God had in mind. As much as we desperately wanted to believe that God would approve of our relationship, in our
"inner parts" the truth had taken root.*

*We fled the MCC church, discerning that the work of darkness was being
presented as light. It was obvious. This experience led us to really face the fact
that our relationship had to change. The time had come for us to agree with
the word of God. If we could not change God's word, God would have to change
us.* □

Penny's sister heard about Regeneration, an Exodus ministry in
Baltimore. Penny and Elaine also received information about a similar ministry in New York City. After they attended a couple of
meetings and heard that they had not been created homosexual, the
truth began to take root in their souls and spirits.

For six years the battle raged on before Penny and Elaine finally
came to a place of complete surrender. At long last they yielded
each other to Jesus. They released one another. They committed

themselves wholeheartedly to God. They each asked God for the gift of celibacy—the ability to be comfortable in refraining from each other sexually. God brought clear understanding that to violate one another would be violating the body of Christ. In January 1984 all sexual activity halted between them, although not easily. Penny describes some of the changes that took place in their lives:

Everything else had changed. Sexual activity had ceased. The desire to have an exclusive relationship was a thing of the past. True godly friendship was forming. It was obvious that if I was not born gay, then I needed to stop affirming that as an identity. In agreement once again with God and one another, we decided to view each other and ourselves as no longer lesbian.

After this deliberate decision of the mind, of course another question arose: Who am I then?

I was no longer attracted in a lesbian way, yet I didn't feel an attraction for the opposite gender. I had to settle with the label "Christian woman." I knew I was a child of God. I identified with Jesus, and he would call me into my true identity. I knew that, through him, I would grow and mature into my heterosexual identity. □

Getting Over Emotional Hurdles

During the difficult process of untangling herself sexually and emotionally from Elaine, Penny read a booklet called *Emotional Dependency*, written by Lori Rentzel. She recalls "finding myself on every page." She began to understand the relational problems she was experiencing and why she was acting in certain ways. At times she was very "bent into" her relationship with Elaine, and she discovered the need to work very hard to stay focused properly—focused on the cross.

As God worked in her heart, Penny discovered within herself an area of misogyny (hatred of women) with which she still occasionally wrestles. From her father she had learned hatred of the feminine, and she was shocked to see how much disdain she held toward herself as a woman as well as toward other women. In fact, this rather strange ambiguity is not uncommon among women who struggle with lesbianism.

The time had come for her to understand how to respond correctly in friendship, in attachments that were built in Christ. All her old responses, all her cravings to have one person meet all her needs had to be surrendered to God.

Even now God continues to show Penny that relationships must be valued in a godly way and worked on daily. God has also taught her to be aware of the enemy's attacks. "I have learned," she says, "that when an emotional wound of the past is opened, God wants to cleanse and heal it. But at the same time, the enemy will attack that vulnerable area and cause chaos. He'll keep it up until I catch on and once again come to Jesus with my bleeding heart and surrender all my emotions to his care."

For Penny, those emotions involved deep and wounded feelings toward both of her parents. When incest was taking place in their home, Penny thought that her mother must have known about it. While Penny was hospitalized during her emotional breakdown, Penny's mother questioned her husband intently. "Did you ever have anything to do with Penny sexually?" she asked repeatedly.

Penny's father denied it emphatically, trying his best to make his wife feel like a fool for thinking such a disgusting thought. Consequently, when her mother finally heard the whole story, a rage of hatred rose up within her. As she witnessed the heat of her mother's anger toward her father, for the first time Penny was aware of her mother's deep love for her. And the first person Penny led to the Lord was her mother.

I was a new Christian and quite evangelistic. I was so excited about Jesus, and no one in my family had a relationship with him. God was so gracious to give me the honor of introducing my mother to her Savior.

Then I prayed about my relationship with my mom and begged God to help me "let go" of my mother and release her to Jesus. I seemed to have this unsatisfied heart cry for connection with her. Now God was showing me the void I was experiencing, and I was beginning to understand why I was so desperate for relationships with women. It was a search for mother love. For years I was clamoring for affection and emotional connection from my mother and always felt empty after being with her.

So at last change began. One time while I was visiting my mother, God began some very deep healing in me. I had not been really looking at my problems with my mother because the pain I was forever aware of and always working on had to do with my father. But one night, because of something we saw on television, she was able to reach out to me warmly and tenderly, acknowledging my deep longing for her.

Afterward I saw my own sin. I had sinned against my mother by demanding that she meet my needs. When God showed me how very little she had received and how little she had to give, I howled in deep repentance. I buckled over in my seat, my head down to my toes.

How gracious of God to show me the poverty of my mother's soul in order to help me understand her inability to nurture me. In this place of utter broken repentance and pain, God set me free. I was cut free from a diseased attachment to my mother. I actually felt a separation in my heart. I felt released. I gained new understanding and therefore had the freedom I needed to stand upright, no longer bent toward my mother. □

A Matter of Life and Death

In February 1982 Penny's father was diagnosed with lung cancer. Chemotherapy started immediately. Her greatest fear was that he would die without Christ. Interestingly, that fear demonstrated to her the depth of forgiveness she had already experienced toward him.

Due to their father's illness Penny's sister came to know the Lord. Penny encouraged her to speak with their dad about her relationship with Christ. One day her sister was in the room talking with him when she called out, "Penny."

When Penny went inside, her sister explained, "Dad just doesn't understand that he needs to ask Jesus into his life in order to get to heaven."

Penny knelt down in front of her father and looked him straight in the eyes—something she had never been able to do. "Pop, what is it you don't understand?"

"I don't believe in hell," he muttered.

They talked for several minutes about the Bible's teaching. "Your spirit will leave your body when you die," she explained, "and you'll be eternally separated from God."

Leaning forward, Penny continued. "Pop, we're a family. We're going to heaven, and we want you with us."

After a moment's thought his face relaxed and softened. Then he said the words Penny had prayed for years to hear: "What do I have to do?"

During the next few minutes Penny and her sister had the glorious honor of leading their dad to the Lord. They prayed with him as he asked for God's forgiveness and accepted Christ as his Savior.

In the coming months Penny was able to see God working within him. Her dad had been a very bitter, angry man. All that anger seemed to fall away as the Lord's Spirit gave him a new calm and peace.

Another important event took place before Penny's father died the following June. He'd never spoken to her about her past lesbian involvement, but she knew that he was ashamed of her. By then the cancer had gone to his brain, and she wasn't really sure he would understand what she was about to say. But it was so heavy on her heart that she had to tell him.

She leaned over him and spoke quietly: "Pop, I never really was the daughter you expected me to be. I'm so sorry about that. Please forgive me."

Her dad gave no visible response, but she continued on anyway: "You weren't the father I expected either. But I've forgiven you. And God's given me such a love for you." Her face was flooded with tears as she kissed his forehead. "I'm so glad we'll be together forever with him."

Today Penny believes that the root issues regarding her lesbianism were intimately related to parental issues that kept her emotionally estranged from her mother and father. As God has revealed various painful areas through the Holy Spirit, the void in her soul has gradually been filled.

More Precious than Gold

On June 9, 1991—Father's Day and the anniversary of her father's death—Penny visited a Sunday evening revival service. As the evening progressed, the Spirit of God moved in a very deep and quiet way. At the close of the service an altar call was given for those seeking refreshing. Penny went forward and was prayed for. As a song was played in the background, the Lord gave her a vision.

The song began, "Lord, You are more precious than silver; Lord, You are more costly than gold." As Penny reflected upon the words, she saw an image of the earth in space. A figure appeared at the horizon, and she recognized that it was Jesus. He came into view, seeming to be within one hundred feet of her, standing off to the right of her focal point. Then another figure appeared on the horizon about two hundred feet away. As this person came forward, Penny realized it was her father. Although she could not clearly see him, she recognized his spirit.

At this point she began to panic. Every fear, every feeling of disgust, of hatred, of anxiety she had ever felt rose up within her. She cried out in her spirit, "Jesus, what is going on here? I thought that I had forgiven my dad. I thought that you'd released me from all of this stuff, from all of the pain, from the sexual abuse, from the violation of trust. Why am I feeling all these feelings again? What is happening?"

At that moment, she heard Jesus say, "I have taken care of it. You are free. I paid the price for your freedom. It is finished."

As soon as she heard those words, the fear left her. She relaxed. All feelings of anxiety fled, replaced by peace. Penny describes what followed:

Suddenly I heard the music again, and I heard myself singing to my father: "Dad, you are more precious than silver; Dad, you are more costly than gold."

As the vision and the music continued, I heard my father singing back to me, "Child, you are more precious than silver; Child, you are more costly than gold."

My heart soared with joy. God brought closure for me in my relationship with my father and comfort after his death by giving me a glimpse of the life he is now experiencing in the heavenly realm.

Happy Father's Day, Pop. □

13

Looking for
One True Friend

Kevin Oshiro

*O*ne of Kevin Oshiro's earliest memories concerns an event that occurred when he was four years old. He was sitting next to the coffee table in the living room of his family's apartment, cutting pages from an old *TV Guide* into strips and then into little tiny squares. He was pretending to be cooking.

Mom was sitting on the couch reading or watching TV or something. Dad came into the room and asked what I was doing. "I'm cooking," I responded. "These are onions, and I'm going to sauté them!"

"That's ridiculous!" Dad exploded. "Girls cook, not boys! What's the matter with you anyway?"

I was furious. I recall Mom trying to make a comment to ease the tension. Dad was mad, and Mom was uncomfortable. But I was furious. □

This incident, which is burned into Kevin's memory, began a

process of detachment from his father that continued well into his adult life. And in Kevin's opinion it became one of five key issues that contributed to his gender confusion and homosexual behavior.

Why did Kevin close his heart to his father at such an early age? He explains, "I couldn't fight back because either I'd get yelled at more or I'd get spanked. So it wouldn't do any good to say anything. Instead what I could do was shut him out of my life. I don't recall how much of a conscious decision that was, but I know that's exactly what happened at that point."

Too Young to Understand

Kevin's fourth year was an eventful one. Around the same time that pivotal incident with his father took place, an eight-year-old male friend sexually molested him, initiating a pattern of sexual activity between the boys that continued into adolescence. These two circumstances left Kevin both with a longing for male affection and with the belief that sex was the evidence of affection.

By the time he reached the third grade, Kevin's sexual encounters included other boys as well. Even at that early age the physical sensation of his encounters was pleasurable and magnified by the excitement of doing something forbidden. It should come as no surprise that somewhere in grade school Kevin started feeling different from other boys. He was simply too young and uninformed to understand what had happened to him.

By junior high, like so many men who struggle with homosexuality, Kevin felt that he was "on the outside looking in." He yearned for a special friend who would somehow cause him to feel secure and valued. His pursuit of such a friendship carried him into several intense, emotionally dependent relationships. But before long he was afraid to approach other boys for sex because his craving now had an ugly name attached to it: *homosexuality*.

Kevin dated girls sporadically in high school and college, but remembers his experiences with girls as being more uncomfortable than fun. He found himself laboring to do what normal guys did, rather than participating in something exciting or desirable. As much as he longed to fit in, he knew that when it came to girls he was going through the motions. The same pattern continued in college. Then, after he had graduated and entered the work force, Kevin's life took a dramatic turn.

One evening I got drunk at an office party, went to an adult bookstore and had a homosexual encounter. I went home disgusted with myself.

"What did I do?" I moaned. The fact that I was excited by the whole experience horrified me most of all. I fought with my sexual desires for another year, then finally confided in my only friend at the time—a lesbian drinking buddy. She enthusiastically introduced me to the gay subculture in Los Angeles. It was January 1982.

I felt happier at first. Capitulating to my desires ended the internal conflict. Now I can be my true self, I thought. But the continual round of drinking, dancing and sex kept me from seeing what homosexuality was doing to my life. The absence of struggling gave me an illusion of freedom.

I thought the excitement of pursuing and being pursued was fulfilling me. In truth, the adrenaline rush numbed my increasing loneliness and quiet desperation to find someone who would really love me. ☐

Kevin quickly became addicted to the excitement of homosexual bars, bookstores and bathhouses. Sex provided a warped sense of adventure. And although the threat of AIDS was all around him, he consciously avoided learning anything about it. Still, he felt that something was missing from his life, something he couldn't exactly identify. Did it have to do with spirituality? With God? At first he wasn't sure.

Searching for Something More

Kevin's grandparents on his father's side were Buddhist, a religion that the family never talked about. Meanwhile, his mother's family was deeply involved in the Salvation Army. His mother had told him stories about his grandfather's ministry as a street preacher and how their family had always reached out to the poor. Even though neither of his parents appeared to have a relationship with God, Kevin vaguely recalled hearing Bible stories, going to daily vacation Bible school as a child and attending an occasional church youth group gathering as a teenager. Still, a personal faith in God had never been a factor in his life.

However, in college one of his best friends was a strong and serious Christian who had shared his spiritual relationship with Kevin. This young man had come to know the Lord in high school and read his Bible and prayed every night before he went to bed.

Several years later, Kevin recalls:

I was miserable enough to try praying. There was no recognition of Jesus in my mind; I merely thought a new job would solve all my problems. God, in his mercy, was drawing me to himself. He began by bringing some new friends into my life.

I soon discovered they were Christians. Weird! *I thought.* Isn't Christianity only for messed-up people who need a crutch? *And yet these folks were neither depressed nor dumb. Instead they had something I hadn't seen before: peace.*

God's peace was something they didn't have to speak about. It was something they were living. It was a part of how they breathed. And I felt from them a strange, unexpected acceptance. Now, granted, I didn't tell them about my involvement with homosexuality. But at that stage it really wasn't important. What was important was that the Lord showed himself to me through their kindness

And even now, as I look back, I think that if I'd needed help, if I'd opened up to talk about anything, they would have been more than willing to listen and help in whatever way they could. But they didn't push anything. They just lived it. □

These friends invited Kevin to join them at a business convention in New Orleans.

It sounded like fun to him, and he went, fully expecting to find some sexual action in that notoriously free-spirited city. But it didn't work out that way. Instead on Saturday evening one of the event coordinators said, "Come to church here at the hotel Sunday morning. It will be the most important thing you do all weekend."

Kevin thought, *Well, I paid my money; it won't hurt to go.* So on Sunday Kevin got dressed and showed up in the hotel ballroom. He isn't sure who spoke or what was said. But at the end of the service the speaker asked, "Do you believe that you're here not by accident but because God caused you to be here?"

Kevin knew that, for him, the answer to that question had to be yes.

"Now," the man continued, "if you'd like to know how to have a personal relationship with Jesus Christ, please come forward and someone will talk with you and explain how you can do that."

That night Kevin asked Jesus to be Lord and Savior of his life. And for some time he continued enjoying a gay lifestyle, making little connection between his new spiritual life and his homosexual behavior. But as he read God's Word and listened to various sermons, it gradually became apparent to Kevin that God's plan for his life did not include homosexuality. And by then he was ready to submit to God.

An Answer to Prayer

"Lord," Kevin prayed, "Your Word says it's wrong, but my feelings tell me otherwise. Please show me what's right, and I'll obey you."

A few days later I went to a midweek service. A young man named Martin testified how God had delivered him from male prostitution.

I was impressed with his story. "I'm gay," I told him after the service. "But I can't do anything about it because I was born this way." Martin showed me some Scriptures about homosexuality. "And such were some of you," he read from 1 Corinthians 6:11.

"Are you familiar with the apostle Paul's conversion?" he asked. "If God can change someone as messed up as Paul, don't you think he can do something in your life?"

I knew then and there that God was answering my prayer for direction.

The next month was awful. Despite my resolution to stay away from the adult bookstores, I continued to give in to my cravings. Finally I snarled at God in frustration: "I can't stand this. What am I supposed to do? I'm trying to change, but I just can't do it!"

"That's exactly right," he said quietly.

Before long God's promise to complete the work he'd begun in my life started to sink in. As Philippians 1:6 says, "He who began a good work in you will carry it on to completion until the day of Christ Jesus." □

Soon after, Kevin found the name of an ex-gay ministry in the back of a book, and they in turn encouraged him to contact a local group called Desert Stream. The group meetings provided a sanctuary for him, a place where he felt safe in talking honestly about his struggles. The program went far beyond everything he'd hoped for or imagined because, little by little, God began healing the relational problems that formed the core of his homosexuality.

And what were those core issues? Kevin identifies five factors that he believes contributed to his sexual confusion.

Factor #1 was the molestation by the older playmate. It crossed a boundary that should only be crossed in adulthood by married couples.

Factor #2 was what Kevin describes as "defensive detachment" from his father. A father, of course, is supposed to be the primary role model of masculinity for a son, but that wasn't the only damage the detachment caused. Isolation caused loneliness, and loneliness heightened his yearning for intimacy. That, in turn, created sexual tension.

Factor #3 was an early, deep emotional wound, inflicted by a female classmate, which caused Kevin to make a vow against trusting or attaching himself emotionally to the opposite sex.

Factor #4 was ethnic shame. When Kevin was a small boy, there were very few Asian families in his neighborhood. Once elementary school started, he became the victim of racial slurs against the Jap-

anese people, which aggravated his sense that there was something
bad about him, something inferior and humiliating.

Factor #5 was an undercurrent of fear that permeated every
aspect of Kevin's self-image. He explains, "There was the sense that
I was not okay as a male. I wasn't athletic, and I felt insecure
around the other boys. As I think about it now, I was just one giant
bundle of fear. And I operated out of this fear for years and years. I
think some of the homosexual attraction, besides being a yearning
to connect with masculinity, was a deep desire to find strength or
identity or power in someone else."

Lessons About Forgiveness

One of the key lessons Kevin learned as he explored his past and
the factors that led him into homosexuality was that because God
had forgiven him, he also needed to forgive those who had
wounded him. The first person who came to mind was his father.

*Forgiveness lays the foundation for a restoration in our relationship with
God. So as I accepted his forgiveness, God also reminded me of a childhood
vow—"I'll never be like Dad"—that was blocking me from accepting my
masculine identity. I renounced these past sins and began experiencing God in
a new way, as a loving Father.*

*At the same time, I had to specifically forgive my father for the different times
I felt he had wronged me. And when I say "forgive," I'm not talking about mini-
mizing anything he did or said, or didn't do or say. I'm talking about releasing
him from my expectations that he acknowledge or make up for the past.*

*Letting go of all that internal demand was freeing. It opened up the door for
me to be able to start seeing my father more as God wanted me to see him.* □

As he reflected on his relationship with his parents, Kevin came
to see that he had always believed that his mother was more supportive than his father. She had been closely involved—sometimes
almost too closely involved—in his life and needs and struggles. But
once the forgiveness process was in place, Kevin realized that his

dad was also very supportive. Although he didn't always have the ability to express his approval or to enjoy himself, his father never missed a band concert or an open house or a parent-teacher conference. "The unfortunate thing was that at the time," Kevin says, "I was blocked. I simply couldn't see it."

Today the relationship with his parents is much different than he could have ever envisioned it.

I genuinely enjoy visiting them. Actually I've had a chance to do a fair amount of that over this past year. I think one of the big differences in our relationship now is that I don't feel a particular need to perform for them. Somewhere along the line it finally sank in that they really loved me apart from my being a "good boy." They really love me, flaws and all. That revelation has given me freedom to enjoy them and not have my defenses on alert.

And the thought of visiting no longer is something that I feel like I've got to psych myself up for. Now I want to be around them. That's especially true as they're getting along in years. I see them slowing down. I see some fragility in them physically that is even a little bit scary. And so it's stirring more desire in me to be around them. □

As Kevin's relationship with his parents improved, as he experienced camaraderie with others who shared his struggle, and as he gained understanding of the things that had driven him, he found the strength to stop having same-sex encounters.

Once he stopped his homosexual behavior, he became obsessed with the fear of relapse. His dread of falling back into sexual addiction was confronted by a friend, who asked him, "Who are you going to put your trust in—your sin or Jesus?"

At that point, Kevin realized that he was no longer a slave to his drives and impulses. There were several close calls that first year, but the temptations were no longer an automatic prelude to sin.

Late in 1987 Kevin moved to the San Francisco area to work for Love In Action, another ex-gay ministry. Before long he joined the Exodus staff and eventually became the conference director, a position he held for three years. He has remained single, and although he has experienced an increasing interest in the opposite sex, he has not yet met a potential life partner. "I'm not seeing anyone *seriously* at the moment. But who knows, maybe that will have changed by the time this book comes out."

The Ongoing Battle with Temptation

Life is not always easy for those who have moved away from homosexual behavior and left the gay life behind. Leading a pure life involves commitment, mental discipline and faithfulness. Kevin lists some of the efforts he's had to make: "Learning how to develop healthy same-sex relationships. Learning boundaries. Repenting of old vows. Repenting of defensive detachment. Being willing to enter into friendships with women and men, and even risking in the area of dating the opposite sex. Getting to a place of self-acceptance."

And have the temptations all gone? Kevin answers:

I'd love to say that they are all vanished and that today I'm the poster child for recovery from homosexuality. But that's not reality. The temptations have changed in that when I first started going to Desert Stream, there was pretty much no lag time between temptation and sin. The temptation was there, and I went out and pursued a contact. Over time, of course, a time-gap developed. It's like I was running toward the edge of the cliff, and, over time, there were more and more fences and barriers helpfully put between the temptation and the cliff.

Today the cliff is still there. And I'm well aware that, like King David, if I'm not where I'm supposed to be and doing what I'm supposed to be doing, I could easily trigger a chain of events where I'm susceptible to going off the deep end, just as David did. If that could happen to him, then it certainly could happen to me. So the lesson is to do all the things I know that are healthy. Staying connected with the Lord. Staying plugged in with friends and church families and avoiding places of temptation. And also, keeping as short a list as I can of grievances.

I think that having to still wrestle a bit is one way that God helps me remain mindful of other people and their weaknesses. Hopefully it helps me to have a little more compassion than I otherwise would have. □

In 1992, following a series of disappointments, Kevin crashed emotionally. He found himself feeling furious with God and with a number of people, and he contemplated rebelling and reverting back to homosexual involvement.

Mentally he evaluated whether, at that time of his life, homosexuality had anything to offer him. How did his new Christian life compare with his former way of life?

"Although Jesus didn't simply wipe away my problems and pain," Kevin said later, "I reached a critical conclusion: as hurt, helpless and angry as I felt, life with the Lord was still better than the best days of pursuing homosexuality."

Today Kevin is working for a high-tech firm in northern California and finds his main ministry in the business world. But he spent a number of years working among those who struggle with homosexual desires and attractions. What would he want to say to those who continue to wrestle with gender issues?

I would pose this question: If the temptations and feelings never completely go away, will you continue to pursue a relationship with the Lord? Are you going to duck out and run? Or are you going to change your theology to accommodate your desires? Is your complete and absolute healing the price tag that God has to pay for your love?

"For he has rescued us from the dominion of darkness and brought us into the kingdom of the Son he loves, in whom we have redemption, the forgiveness of sins" (Colossians 1:13-14).

He reminds us through his Word, his Spirit and other people that none of us qualifies for some elite rank among sinners. He also reminds us that we are saints by his mercy and adopted children by his kindness.

Today I'm experiencing security, purpose and genuine love through Jesus Christ. He has become the true friend I looked for—but never found—in the gay community.

Will he be anything less to you? □

14

Free Indeed

Barbara Swallow

*T*he snowflakes were growing larger. Floating bits of white fluff filled the air, as if someone had ripped open a feather pillow. Barbara Swallow—a fifty-four-year-old wife and mother struggling with lesbianism—peered out the window and trembled uncontrollably.

Later, while praying about this mindless fear, Barbara saw something, someone, with the eyes of her spirit: a frightened three-year-old girl standing in a cloud of white feathers. A white rooster landed at her feet with a thud, then staggered around like a drunken thing. And there was Barbara's uncle, standing in front of the little girl, holding a baseball bat.

Suddenly the adult Barbara remembered everything. *She* was that little girl. Her uncle and she were in her grandfather's yard, and his prize rooster had just been hit by a baseball bat. The child Barbara had panicked. Suddenly her uncle had scooped her up and taken her to the cellar, where he had molested her. Afterward, he'd warned, "Don't you ever tell anyone what happened today!"

Two years after the molestation by her uncle, another horrifying story unfolded in Barbara's life. Her mother began drawing her into her bed to molest Barbara, which she continued to do until Barbara was nearly eight.

As a child the only times I remember being given individual attention by my mother were when I played the male role in her bed. Unconsciously, I began to accept the idea that my value rested in my sexual capabilities. Perhaps, if I could function as a boy, I would be loved and would prove myself to be of some merit.

I don't know what caused my mother to do what she did. She has passed away now, so I can only speculate. I do remember, however, noticing a change in my mother's personality after one particular event. Perhaps her inability to finish grieving over that incident is what led to such incongruous behavior and neglect.

When I was around four years old, I distinctly remember my mother going to the hospital to have a baby. I remember just as distinctly that she came home without a baby. No one ever explained this, and I must have simply assumed she and Dad had decided not to have a baby after all. Still, I could not understand why Mom got so angry whenever we tried to play with that lovely, double-sized baby carriage in the basement.

Mom changed after that. Dad changed too. All of our lives seemed to take a turn for the worse from then on.

Within a year we moved to a house in the country. Mom spent most of her time in bed. She stopped getting up every mealtime to feed us. She would get up to make Dad's dinner, but the only times I remember having the table set and food fixed for us kids were once or twice a year when the extended family got together for some holiday. Even then it was a traumatic episode for my mother because she absolutely hated entertaining. My sister, Pat, who was then about eleven years old, pretty much took care of my brother and me from then on. Mom was too depressed to get involved. ☐

Barbara's molestation by her uncle (which she was unable to

remember for five decades) and her mother's subsequent abuses convinced Barbara that it really wasn't safe to be a girl.

Finding a New Identity

From age five on, Barbara's parents ignored her, and she fended for herself in order to eat. Her mother showed abhorrence for anything female. She hated housework and cooking, and she did not nurture her children. Because no one loved Barbara the way she was, she constructed a new, masculine identity. She played with her brother and his friends, thoroughly enjoying their company and their games.

She found some acceptance—or, at least, some attention—from her father whenever she displayed any evidence of masculinity. So Barbara worked hard to develop her physical strength. She stopped thinking of herself as a girl and, in her own mind, she became a "neutral" person. She recalls:

Between the ages of nine and thirteen I began to be the son my father had always wanted. Dad and I never developed any real closeness, but I was able to spend time in my father's presence by helping him with manual labor around the house. My brother was never interested in the things my dad wanted him to do. So when Dad began fulfilling his lifelong dream of building a house, I became his colaborer. I did carpentry work and mixed concrete and hauled cinderblocks right alongside my dad. He even got in the habit of calling me "Bob" instead of Barbara.

By that time I was living in jeans, T-shirts and sneakers. There was no dress code, but this was in the early 1950s, and most girls my age still wore skirts to school. I no longer thought of myself as a girl, however. I preferred thinking of myself as just a neutral sort of person.

Everything seemed to conspire against me being happy as a girl. When I had been a boy for my mother, she noticed me. In school I was required to dress and act like a girl. And yet, while trying to play that role, I was cruelly and definitively rejected. At home or at school, playing a girl's role didn't get me praise; it brought me slavery and torment.

And so, the stage was set. I was ready to be noticed. But who would pay attention to me? It wasn't long before I stopped trying to be the girl God had created me to be and chose instead to seek another path toward acceptance, love and belonging. □

A New Life with Ronald . . . and Marla

During high school Barbara conformed outwardly to her teenage peers, dating and participating in girl talk. The behavior kept her from looking on the outside as different as she felt on the inside.

Boys were fascinating to other girls but not to her. She knew what boys were like, inside and out. But girls? Girls were mysterious and intriguing. Barbara did not understand what made them so soft and gentle. All that lacked nurturing within her was drawn to her secret, carefully hidden hope that she would somehow, someday be lavished with feminine attention.

Still, Barbara did not give in to her ever-intensifying attractions to women until after she married her husband, Ronald. Before long the couple had a new baby son, and soon Barbara found herself trapped in all the female responsibilities that she loathed.

Then along came Marla. Marla poured out attention on Barbara, and she was more than willing to help with everyday household tasks like cleaning and cooking. Before long the two women had slipped into a lesbian relationship, which they kept hidden for the next sixteen years. Barbara indulged all her pent-up feelings with zeal. But whenever she emerged from the bedroom with Marla, she came away empty.

Almost as soon as my relationship with Marla began, Ronald began tying himself up with work and union activities. He seemed to be losing interest in the things of the Lord, and he stopped making time for God. Without realizing it, he had let go of the very cord that had connected me to him in the first place.

With Marla's help at home, things seemed to be running like clockwork; there was no worry for him there. Marla was busy taking care of me, so

Ronald was relieved of that confusing responsibility. And, as often happens when things seem to be going well, no one saw any reason to bother asking God for advice. No one was aware of any danger. No one saw the ugly storm on the horizon. No one was prepared for its fury.

On working days my time with Ron was in the afternoon, when he came home from work. Our memories differ somewhat on what our relationship was like during that time. Ronald and I were great in bed, but we were connected only by sex. We talked about the kids, the money or the weather, but we didn't talk in depth about anything. Not being included in any serious dialogue with him made me feel like an unintelligent, unimportant knickknack on his shelf. I didn't feel Ronald saw me as capable of supplying relevant input for important decisions. I didn't see my opinions being sought out or valued. I didn't believe that my husband esteemed me.

Although Marla gave me a certain amount of emotional support, it wasn't long before she started belittling my opinions and putting me down. She began to treat me with the same disregard as Ronald did. Sometimes, when the three of us were together and there was a ballgame on TV, Ron and Marla would be on the couch, laughing and joking and enjoying the game together, while I was completely left out. I felt forgotten by both of them. It was a reenactment of my fifth year of life. □

Barbara had two more children. After each birth Marla got more jealous and violent. She began to dominate Barbara's life, threatening the lives of Barbara's children if she talked about leaving Marla. She also threatened to tell Ronald about the lesbian relationship if Barbara so much as signed a birthday card to him with the word *love*. Barbara was a victim again—this time of emotional blackmail.

Marla had begun to sexually abuse Barbara. Before long the abuse became so intense that a doctor told Barbara that she would need to undergo a hysterectomy. By this time she had experienced an emotional breakdown and had tried to commit suicide. Yet, strangely, as she anticipated this surgery, she was terrified of dying.

Hope from Heaven

Meanwhile, Barbara's fifteen-year-old son had gone to a religious
retreat and had come home born again, bubbling over with the
Spirit of God. Ron Jr. was aglow with joy and peace. He told his
mother that she had nothing to fear even in death if she had Jesus
in her heart. Then he took her to his prayer group where she saw
other teens singing and praying with joyful exuberance that made
her yearn for the same kind of openness with God.

*Later, in the hospital awaiting the hysterectomy, I was like a crazy person,
wanting to take communion like some people throw salt over their shoulder—
just in case. By then I was unable to claim a personal faith of my own, so I
thought maybe doing communion would be as acceptable to God as real belief
in him.*

Minutes ticked away but no one could find a priest.

*Then, unexpectedly, a peaceful feeling came over me. Just before the sur-
gery was to begin, I suddenly understood. God stepped in and rescued me. As if
I was too small to reach the light switch, like a loving father God saw his child
stumbling around in the dark. He reached out over my head quietly and
clicked on the light for me. And right there, on the gurney outside the operat-
ing room, I made a decision.*

*Later I wrote in my journal: "How very strange that I could have received
Jesus into my little heart so long ago and yet never really gotten to know who
he is. But now, suddenly, in the twinkling of an eye I know him. Before, I
accepted the fact that Jesus had died for mankind. Today, I realize he came
and died for me.*

"Yesterday, I knew he was the Savior. Today, he is my Savior.

*"Yesterday, I understood that he is Lord of all the earth. Today, I take him
as Lord of my little life.*

*"I receive him with open and such grateful arms, full of relief. I no longer
want my life. I'm tired of it. I want his life. I can't make mine work, but for
some strange reason, he wants to take it and make something of it."* □

In the following weeks Barbara craved the Bible. Like a starving person she feasted on its words, and they began to fill a vast hole inside her spirit that nothing had ever filled before.

But for the first time, as she read Barbara discovered that God did not like homosexuality. Those were shocking words to read. How could she change who she was? Immediately she resolved to stop her lesbian behavior. But it took a year of prayer and support from Jeanne, a good friend, before she summoned the courage she would need to break off with Marla. And it took another year of fear, of threats, of continuing abuse before she finally found the courage to reach out for help.

To my surprise, the priest not only came immediately, but he talked with me for two full hours. At last he told me that I had no choice. My very soul was at stake here. I knew that by taking action, I could lose everything—my marriage, my kids, my home. But I was no longer willing to live in hell or to risk my soul. The very next day I would have to tell Marla to leave.

I had made a decision. I would not turn back. But it had to be done quickly, while I still had the courage. I called Marla and asked her to come to the house. She sat down opposite me, but I remained standing. Without emotion, I told her I wanted her out.

"Excuse me? What do you mean 'out'?"

" 'Out,' as in 'out the door,' 'out of my life,' 'leave and don't come back.' I don't ever want to see you again."

She tried to console me, tried to argue with me, but when she really grasped that I was serious, she began to cry. She slumped onto the floor in a heap, sobbing. "Please don't send me away. We can just be friends. I'll be good."

Fortunately, the priest had warned me not to listen to any arguments, not to pay attention to any tears, just to stand my ground. This I did. I was like a robot, without feeling, without emotion. I couldn't have afforded to feel sorry for her or to regret what I was doing. All would be lost if I did. I felt like I was watching the whole scene through another person's eyes. I couldn't believe that I was actually the one doing this.

In a remarkably short time Marla gave up pleading and left. She attempted in various ways to get back into my life. She tried joining the prayer group that met at Jeanne's house, but Jeanne warned me whenever she was coming, and I stayed home. Jeanne and her husband sincerely tried to minister to Marla, but she soon quit coming to their home. □

Even after the breakup, however, Barbara's desires did not change. Again her friend Jeanne was indispensable, supporting her as she fought waves of temptation, guilt and disappointment.

A Confession and a New Beginning

Finally, in 1988 when she was fifty-four, God appointed a day of deliverance for Barbara. A few days after the "panic in the snow," when she recalled the molestation by her uncle, Barbara spent twenty-four hours in prayer with another Christian friend. During that prayer session God pulled out all the old demons that had controlled and distorted Barbara's thoughts and emotions for so many years. The change was evident the very next day. She and her friend went to the mall to relax after the intense time in prayer. Suddenly she realized, in utter surprise, that for the first time in her life, she was noticing not women but men. Something had changed. Something very deep.

After her encounter with the past and the healing that followed, Barbara realized that she had to tell her husband about her lesbian struggles. In her journal, she wrote:

Today I told Ronald about my past. That sounds like it was easy, but it was one of the hardest—no, the hardest thing I have ever had to do.

Ronald found me sitting, looking out the window toward the mountains. I was crying and sobbing. I knew the Lord was asking me to reveal my past to Ronald, but before I felt I was ready to begin, Ronald walked in on me.

I tried to brush him off when he asked me what was wrong. But I hadn't had time to wipe the tears away, and I was obviously a wreck, so Ronald wouldn't take "nothing" as an acceptable answer. When he pressed for an answer, I just cried all the louder.

"Come on, now. How bad can it be?"

I said, "It's not about now, but it's about the past."

"How bad can it be? Did you have an affair or something?"

"No, it's worse than that!" I cried hysterically.

"Tell me what's wrong. I want to know."

"Okay. It's about Marla. She and I ... I was a lesbian, but ... it's hard to talk about it. ... Please forgive me! Please don't leave me!"

The next moment was the most incredible of all my life. I saw Ronald stand before me and spread his arms out from side to side, beckoning me. "I forgive you. It's in the past. I love you very much."

I was in his arms before I remember getting up, and there I stayed. Together we cried and cried and cried.

When we could talk again, we began to share with each other as we had never shared before. I told him about my uncle and what had happened. I told him about the healing that the Lord had done in my life. For the first time I was able to rejoice with Ronald over the miracle that had happened, about being free at last. I never realized how much I needed to share my victories with Ronald.

Ronald wanted to know everything. No more secrets. He wanted to know so that he would never do anything that would remind me of the past or hurt me in any way. □

The freedom to tell Ronald everything was matched only by the freedom Barbara experienced when God delivered her in the mountains. Until she confided in her husband, she was sure she would lose him if he ever found out about her homosexual behavior. Instead, after Ronald opened his arms and forgave Barbara, he also encouraged her to tell her story, to share her healing with others who struggle with similar gender-related temptations. Despite initial reluctance on the part of some of their children, Barbara and Ronald persevered. Today they minister as a team, helping others find their way out of homosexuality through the power and love of Jesus.

Like Barbara's, our ideas are pretty well fixed by our early experiences in life. Before we have had an opportunity to compare our lives with others, we've drawn conclusions about families, our life and ourselves in general. A mother doesn't *normally* require sexual favors of her daughter. *Normally,* a father is able to accept and treat his daughter as female. *Normally,* love and acceptance aren't bought and sold. But these were all part and parcel of Barbara's life, and she knew nothing different until she was married, a mother and a lesbian.

Barbara says today that she knew what gratification felt like but not satisfaction. She knew how to fight for acceptance but not how to find it. She wanted to be loved, yet she never seemed able to earn that love. She didn't know what was wrong in her life, but she was desperately unhappy. Year after year, toiling for love, she wearied of life itself. Barbara cannot envision what her life would be like today if God had not intervened. She writes to others who are trying to cope with gender confusion and homosexual behavior:

I want to encourage you, to let you know that Jesus truly heals lesbianism and homosexuality. There is more available to you than just abstinence, more than struggling with temptation for the rest of your life. Jesus can set you free from every aspect of your unhealthy thought patterns and from all the junk that goes with them.

Don't be afraid to let Jesus into the painful areas of your life. Allow him to walk through them with you. With Christ's help, force yourself through the pain.

I know at times it is so tempting to try and avoid feeling the pain of the past because when we feel it, it's just as real as if it were happening all over again. But just think, if you trust Jesus, he can heal the hurt, and you will never have to live with that pain again. Just imagine the freedom.

When you push through the past with Jesus Christ, he can heal you forever.

I assure you that he is able to do this.

He did it for me. □

Afterword

One of the current discussions among Exodus leaders is the question, "What does 'change' mean for the homosexual?" Now that you have read these fourteen stories, you can better understand why this is such a topic of discussion. "Change" means many different things, depending on whose story is being considered. Change *is* real, but it is not the same in every case.

Some ex-gay men and women are virtually free of homosexual thoughts and feelings; others continue to experience same-sex attractions to varying degrees. All of them, however, have one thing in common: they all reject *gay* and *lesbian* as the central defining aspect of their personhood. And all of them have experienced major changes in their lives. They are *not* the same men and women they were ten years ago—or even last year.

Making the Change
If you are exploring the possibility of leaving homosexuality—or if you have already begun that transition process—we hope that these stories have been instructive and encouraging. You have probably noticed a few common themes throughout this book. One of the most important is that this kind of life-altering decision to leave homosexuality is often motivated by a faith-based desire to please

God and live in accordance with his plan for our lives.

Leaving homosexuality is impossible in your own strength. If you have never considered God's desire to be an active part of your life, please contact Exodus (<info@exodusnorthamerica.org>) for more information on how you can enter into a new life based on a personal relationship with Jesus Christ. And, if you have already begun your Christian journey but are bogged down with distractions and discouragement, we can put you in touch with an Exodus ministry in your area whose staff will walk alongside you in the process of change and spiritual growth.

A Word to Family Members and Friends

We also know that this book will find its way into the hands of many people with a gay loved one. To you, we have some words of instruction based on the stories you have just read. You may have noticed that in many cases family members have played a pivotal role in an individual's decision to leave homosexuality. However, ultimately, you cannot make that decision for another person. Your adult friend or relative must decide the direction of his or her future. It is outside of your direct control. But you can be an influence through prayer, encouragement and speaking "the truth in love" as the Spirit of God guides you.

This book is one way that you can influence another person. Consider passing along a copy to anyone who is interested in the possibility of leaving homosexuality. Personal testimonies are a powerful witness. ("If it happened to them, maybe it could happen to me.") Above all, pray for God's Spirit to persuade, convict and draw your loved one to himself. His power is infinite, and his love is life changing.

Many, many people contact Exodus for advice on dealing with gay family members and friends. We always tell them the same thing: "Share with them the good news that change is possible—then leave the decision up to them. And, whatever they do, overwhelm them with unconditional love."

If You Are Seeking Change

We want to close with a word of encouragement to anyone seeking freedom from homosexuality. We pray that God will abundantly bless you as you pursue his best for your life. We know from experience that being in the center of his will is the place of ultimate joy and peace. Don't settle for second best.

Remember the prayer we mentioned in the introduction to this book? "Lord, make me into the woman (or man) of God that you created me to be." May that prayer be yours on a daily basis. And may your portrait be added to the thousands of others who grace God's heavenly gallery of men and women who have forsaken the old ways to embrace his path of new life and victory.

For information on an ex-gay ministry in your area, contact Exodus International North America at

P.O. Box 77652, Seattle, WA 98177
Phone: (206) 784-7799
Fax: (206) 784-7872
E-mail: info@exodusnorthamerica.org
World Wide Web: www.exodusnorthamerica.org

Outside North America, go online to <www.exodusinternational.org> and click on your continent on the world map for information on your regional Exodus office.